FERTILITY HOLIDAYS

Fertility Holidays

IVF Tourism and the Reproduction of Whiteness

Amy Speier

NEW YORK UNIVERSITY PRESS

New York

NEW YORK UNIVERSITY PRESS
New York
www.nyupress.org

References to Internet websites (URLs) were accurate at the time of writing. Neither the author nor New York University Press is responsible for URLs that may have expired or changed since the manuscript was prepared.

Library of Congress Cataloging-in-Publication Data
Names: Speier, Amy, author.
Title: Fertility holidays : IVF tourism and the reproduction of whiteness / Amy Speier.
Description: New York : New York University Press, 2016. | Includes bibliographical references and index.
Identifiers: LCCN 2015043574 | ISBN 978-1-4798-2766-4 (cl : alk. paper) | ISBN 978-1-4798-4910-9 (pb : alk. paper)
Subjects: LCSH: Medical tourism.
Classification: LCC RA793.5 .S66 2016 | DDC 362.1—dc23
LC record available at http://lccn.loc.gov/2015043574

New York University Press books are printed on acid-free paper, and their binding materials are chosen for strength and durability. We strive to use environmentally responsible suppliers and materials to the greatest extent possible in publishing our books.

Manufactured in the United States of America

10 9 8 7 6 5 4 3 2 1

Also available as an ebook

To Wes

CONTENTS

Acknowledgments   ix

Introduction   1

1. From Hope to Alienation: North Americans Enter the
   Baby Business   17

2. Virtual Communities and Markets   41

3. Intimate Labor within Czech Clinics   63

4. Contradictions of Fertility Holidays   101

5. Separate but Connected Paths   118

   Conclusion: An Eye to the Future   143

   Notes   151

   Bibliography   153

   Index   163

   About the Author   167

ACKNOWLEDGMENTS

Because this book has been a long time in the making, there are many people I need to thank. First, I want to thank Joan Marler for sending me the link about fertility holidays; I bet she had no idea how important that was for my career trajectory! I appreciate the support of the National Science Foundation for funding this research and Deborah Winslow's astute directorship of the program over the course of my research.

I must credit my graduate school advisers from the University of Pittsburgh, who continue to be important mentors and friends. I feel lucky to have had Joseph Alter as my graduate adviser, and I can finally call him Joe. I also want to thank Robert Hayden, Nicole Constable, and Andrew Strathern for their guidance. To my amazing graduate school cohort and friends—Leah Voors, Frayda Cohen, Claudia Petruccio, Sarah Thurston, Angela Lockard, Elissa Helms, Neringa Klumbyte, and Edgardo Ruiz—I appreciate all of you.

Special thanks goes out to those involved in the reproductive travel industry in the Czech Republic, including the IVF brokers, marketers, clinicians, coordinators, and nurses. Since I cannot name you individually, please know that I am indebted to your willingness to let me linger in your waiting rooms and offices for several summers. I also appreciate the pension owners that urged me to consider it a home while I was there for several months.

Of course, I am most heavily indebted to those couples and women who have shared with me their intimate experiences with infertility and their attempts at creating a family. Please know that I am forever grateful for your thoughtful conversations over the past several years. Thank you for letting me into your homes. I hope that I have captured your experiences in my rendering; any deficiencies are mine alone.

Just as this book is multisited, my own career has been multisited throughout this project. The seeds were planted while I was a postdoctoral fellow at Lawrence University. There, I was lucky to have Jenna Stone's individual, specialized grant-writing knowledge to guide the grant proposal process. Upon moving to Eckerd College, my first point of contact was the lovely Iris Yetter, who helped me put the final touches on my revised proposal. I was granted the National Science Foundation award for the summer of 2010 and enjoyed two full summers of research while I was at Eckerd. Subsequently, I transitioned to a new position at the University of Texas at Arlington in the summer of 2012. During that summer, I had the pleasure of following up with couples all over North America while on a fabulous road trip with Debbie Bensadon.

At the University of Texas at Arlington, I have joined several variations of writing groups. I am particularly indebted to my two senior colleagues Christian Zlolniski and Heather Jacobson, who read several drafts of every chapter for this book. They always provided astute guidance and supportive feedback. I have enjoyed meeting Dustin Harp, an amazing friend and like-minded colleague, once a week at coffee shops throughout the Dallas–Fort Worth area. She was generous enough to read a draft of the first half of the book. Burcu Bayram has been a daily advocate whose shared Google Docs and happy hours have been tremendously helpful. Thank you all for being my advocates.

I am blessed with friends who are scattered all over the world, and I feel so very lucky to have their emotional and intellectual support. I have enjoyed casual conversations about my research with more people than I can possibly remember, though I do recall running through the layout and outline with Jenny Keefe at a brewery in Chicago. For now, I thank my Eckerd colleagues Lauren Highfill Symmes, Karen Pitcher Christianson, Kathleen Keller, Heather Vincent (world's best mentor), Andy and Katie Ewing, Zachary Dobbins, and Tracye Keen,

I have enjoyed reading the work of other medical anthropologists engaged in similar research projects of various strands of reproductive travel. A special thanks to the participants of the Cambridge Round Table: Marcia Inhorn, Zeynep Gürtin, Giulia Zanini, Andrea Whittaker, Amrita Pande, and Richard Storrow.

Thank you to the generous reviewers for your helpful comments and enthusiasm. I have presented various versions of this book at too many conferences to list here. Special thanks go to Susan Frohlick, Frayda Cohen, Amrita Pande, and Yasmine Ergas.

From the first moment of pitching my book idea to Jennifer Hammer of NYU Press at the American Anthropological Association meetings in Chicago in the fall of 2013, she has been immediately available, efficient, and professional in working with me. Thank you for guiding me through this process.

Introduction

In my small bed-and-breakfast room in Moravia, I interviewed April, a blonde, blue-eyed music educator, and her husband, Larry, a teddy bear of a man. The two sat side by side, squished on my maroon leather loveseat, as I perched across from them on the edge of my bed. They took turns answering my questions about their experience with infertility and the world of assisted reproduction. The ease and flow of the conversation indicated a close, loving relationship and their mutual support. High school sweethearts, April and Larry were ready to have a baby once they had been married several years. After a year of seeing what would happen when they stopped using contraception, they began to wonder. April started charting her temperature to find out when she ovulated, and they began having "timed relations." After another six months of making a more concerted effort, April decided to speak to her ob-gyn. Sadly, they learned that Larry had "weak" sperm, and they were referred to a fertility specialist.

April and Larry were frustrated at what they felt was an interruption in their planned life cycle. Larry's low sperm count affected his sense of masculinity, while April panicked because she had always wanted children. As they watched the families of their close friends grow, they felt increasingly isolated in their struggles. April joined an online support group for infertility called RESOLVE, where she basked in the support and information shared among women.

At the fertility clinic, the doctor suggested April and Larry begin with noninvasive intrauterine injections (IUIs) to give Larry's sperm a "jump start." They underwent three cycles of IUI, at which point they decided that April should take fertility drugs to help stimulate the growth of more eggs, aiming to increase chances for conception. After another three unsuccessful rounds of IUI, their doctor suggested they begin to think seriously about in vitro fertilization (IVF).

The doctor sent April and Larry to the clinic's business office, which handled payment issues. The woman at the business office tallied the costs of future office visits at $300 per visit, the various procedures they would need, such as intracytoplasmic sperm injection (ICSI),[1] and costly medications. With only partial insurance coverage, they found themselves having to pay for nearly everything out of pocket. The price tag kept climbing until it reached $15,000. The two of them decided to put off renovating their bathroom and dipped into their savings.

When their first cycle was unsuccessful, the doctor suggested they try IVF using donor egg, which again increases the chance of conception. But the price tag for IVF using an egg donor skyrocketed to nearly $35,000. Their jaws dropped, and they felt like a concrete road barrier had crashed in front of them, ending all chances for a semibiological family. They knew they could not afford it. The clinic suggested that they remortgage their house. Once again, April, heartbroken, turned to her online support group.

A fellow RESOLVE member told April about a company called IVF Holiday that was arranging IVF with donor egg in the Czech Republic at dramatically lower prices. At first, April thought traveling so far away was a crazy idea, and she dismissed it immediately. But she kept returning to the IVF Holiday website, reading testimonials about couples' successful IVF cycles. The website proffered images of smiling white babies as well as beautiful European landscapes, claiming couples would have "plenty of time to see exactly what you want and leave with wonderful experiences." One day she contacted IVF Holiday, whose owners gave her contact information for previous clients, whom she called to speak with about their experiences. April knew she could convince Larry to go abroad, simply because the price would be a third of the price of an IVF cycle at home. Also, they had always talked about traveling around Europe. Once again, April and Larry began to be excited about the prospect of trying to have a baby.

April sent her medical history to the IVF broker, who arranged all their clinical appointments. Larry and April were assured they would be picked up at the airport and taken to a small town in Moravia where the clinic was located. They decided to stay at a pension, a small bed-and-breakfast. April and Larry were stunned by the dramatically lower costs of the medications they received in the mail from the Czech clinic. As April began her medications, Larry perused travel websites, fantasizing about trips to Prague or Vienna with thoughts of romantic castles on his mind. They were riding on clouds of hope.

Early in June 2010, April and Larry flew to Prague, Czech Republic, where they met another couple—Jessica and Doug—who arrived the same day, rode with them to the eastern Czech town, and stayed in the same small, intimate pension, where they ate breakfast together every day for three weeks. During their stay in the Czech Republic, April and Jessica visited the clinic together and even had their embryo transfers the same day. The two couples shared stories of trying to get pregnant as they explored local attractions together.

April and Larry were pleasantly surprised by the friendly owners of the bed-and-breakfast, a small family whose kindness and generosity were unsurpassed. They felt respected by the Czech doctors, whose names seemed unpronounceable but who spent a lot of time answering their questions, never rushing them. They felt like they had a navigator in their IVF brokers, who showed they truly cared by checking on them while they were in the Czech Republic. Everyone seemed to want April to get pregnant.

Larry surprised April by booking a four-star hotel in Prague, directly under the castle, as a last splurge before heading home, hoping for pregnancy. They dined on the rooftop, serenaded by a quartet playing Dvořák and Smetana. April felt like a queen and was optimistic. She thought the music must be soothing to the two embryos recently transferred into her uterus. April and Larry were sad to say good-bye to Jessica and Doug, and the women vowed to stay in touch and keep track of one another's progress. They joked that maybe their roads would cross once again if they decided to return to the Czech Republic for another round of IVF, trying for siblings of their future babies. Sadly, April and Larry's cycle was not successful this time,[2] although Jessica and Doug welcomed twin boys the following spring.

Fertility Tourism?

This is the story of a North American couple I met, who, like so many others, encountered financial barriers to accessing fertility treatment at home. Reproductive travel, what Briggs (2010:51) has referred to as "offshore (re)production," has grown as one of the main forms of medical travel due to the high cost of infertility treatment in the United States (Spar 2006; C. Thompson 2005); the unavailability of gamete donors, as in Germany (Bergmann 2011); strict regulatory laws, as in Italy (Zanini 2011); or a lack of general access to biomedical technologies, as in Nigeria (Pennings 2002). Given the global scope of reproductive travel, there is a "wide range of very different forms of regulation, bans, and approvals as well as considerable differences in clinical practice, public or private financing, and moral or ethical reasoning" (Knecht, Klotz, and Beck 2012:12).

Scholars have debated the terminology of fertility tourism, referring to it as "reproductive tourism," "procreative tourism," or "cross-border reproductive care" (Gürtin and Inhorn 2011; Whittaker and Speier 2010). Franklin has called it "reproductive trafficking" (2012:34), and many qualify the word "tourism" with quotation marks. The majority of scholars find the term problematic, since it connotes pleasure "and thus trivializes fertility problems" (Knoll 2012:265). Some argue that in the case of same-sex couples or unmarried individuals the label "reproductive exiles" is more appropriate, since they are forced to seek treatment abroad (Matorras 2005; Inhorn and Patrizio 2009). Most assume it is the wealthy who can afford to travel abroad for medical care, yet Elisa Sobo and her collaborators claim that "medical travelers seeking biomedical treatment overseas may be disproportionately representative of the working poor" (2011:133). Admittedly, because infertile couples are otherwise healthy, "IVF treatment *can* lend itself to a combination of treatment and tourism between appointments" (Whittaker and Speier 2010:370).

I argue that since IVF Holidays are branded as vacations, the "tourism" terminology should be retained. Knoll is in agreement when she writes, "From my anthropological perspective, tourism is an analytic term that captures the complexities of various kinds of peaceful movements across borders" (2012:265) and, more specifically, that "the notion of reproductive tourism therefore captures new forms of choice and consumerism in health care that tend to undermine the distinction between tourism and health care" (267). Whatever term used, it is a phenomenon enabled by globalization and the commercialization of reproductive medicine (Gürtin and Inhorn 2011).

The multitude of reproductive travel routes is "varied"; a recent symposium on cross-border reproductive care includes twenty-two nations and five continents (Gürtin and Inhorn 2011). Ironically, the United States is a destination site because of the scant amount of regulation, though laws do vary from state to state. California is a favorite destination for gay couples, as well as for surrogacy—but it is largely for the wealthy elite, with the cost of treatments estimated at $100,000. Typically, however, destination sites of fertility travel can offer medical infrastructure and expertise, certain regulatory frameworks, and lower wage structures, which allow reproductive technologies to be performed at competitive, lower costs. In addition to a sense of cultural familiarity (which may mean a common language), patients are often seeking specific services such as sex selection, surrogacy, or commercial ova donation (Blyth and Farrand 2005).

Given the global scope of reproductive tourism, as well as the methodological complexities of tracing these travel routes, data are fragmented regarding this "patchwork of widely diverging national laws" (Klotz and Knecht 2012:284). It is impossible to know how many people are traveling internationally for this type of care (Nygren et al. 2010). There are well-established "hubs" of reproductive tourism. India is known for its surrogacy market, offering some of the most affordable cycles at $20,000. Thailand is a hot spot for couples wanting to select the sex of their offspring using preimplantation genetic diagnosis (PGD) on embryos (Whittaker 2011). Other areas of the globe involved in reproductive travel are South Africa, Mexico, and the United States.

A reported 24,000 to 30,000 cycles of IVF are performed in Europe each year, serving 11,000 to 14,000 patients (Inhorn and Patrizio 2012). The Czech Republic is emerging as one of the top European destinations for reproductive travel because, unlike most countries, it offers anonymous egg donation. Spain is the largest and oldest provider of reproductive medicine to foreign patients, and the Czech industry largely mimics the Spanish model in terms of regulations. However, the Czech Republic presently has "gaps" in regulations. Bergmann has named these "two of the main European destinations for egg donation" (2012:333).

There are 200 clinics in Spain, which attests to the fact that reproductive travel has been an established industry for much longer than in the Czech Republic. In addition, since 2006 Spanish clinics may not discriminate against any person as a potential client, whereas the 43 Czech clinics will treat only married heterosexual couples. Because the Czech Republic's population is largely atheist, limiting treatment to couples is related not to religious belief but rather to heteronormative state policies.

Czech clinical websites advertise in English, German, Italian, and Russian, promising a ready availability of student egg donors with only a three-month waiting period. The Czech reproductive medical field is profiting from its lower price structure and liberal legislation stipulating that sperm and egg donation must be voluntary and anonymous. Donors cannot be paid for their eggs but are offered attractive "compensatory payments" of approximately 1,000 euros ($1,134) for the discomfort involved in ovarian stimulation and oocyte retrieval. For North American patients traveling to the Czech Republic during the time of this research, treatment for IVF was $3,000, and for an egg donor cycle the cost was $4,000. North Americans spend, on average, $10,000 for the entire trip to the Czech Republic. In comparison, a round of IVF with egg donation in the United States costs between $25,000 and $40,000.

The European reproductive medical industry oriented toward foreign patients seems to be expanding eastward, as several Eastern European countries have recently emerged in this global market with slight differences in regulation. The Ukraine allows for "virtually everything," including surrogacy, while Bulgaria does not have legislation about surrogacy yet (Global IVF 2012). Like the Czech Republic, Hungary restricts clients to heterosexual couples. However, if a single woman suffers from a medical condition like cancer that requires chemotherapy, which will likely lead to infertility, a clinic in Hungary will allow her to undergo IVF. Romania used to provide gamete donation for foreigners, until the practice was outlawed in 2008 (Nahman 2013).

The global market of reproductive technologies as painted here obviously offers a vast array of choices for patients aiming to create a family using reproductive technologies. As North Americans are shopping the globe for different destination countries, they are acting as consumers with respect to their health care. One objective of this book is to trace North American quests for parenthood along this global care route to the Czech Republic.

Most assume that this phenomenon of reproductive travel needs no further explanation beyond cost-effectiveness. However, as consumers, North Americans do not decide to travel abroad only for lower prices: indeed, the Czech Republic does not offer the lowest prices in the market. Thus, much more needs to be understood about this recent phenomenon because it reveals the complex interplay between global neoliberal shifts in health care and individual experiences of reproductive travel. The existence of the global care chain between North America and the Czech Republic can be credited to two entrepreneurial Czech women, Hana and Petra, both of whom married American men and subsequently suffered infertility. Both transnational couples had been "return reproductive travelers" (Inhorn 2011) to their Moravian hometowns in the Czech Republic, where they had access to state-funded assisted reproductive technologies (ARTs). After receiving treatment, each woman created an IVF broker agency, hoping to help other North Americans unable to afford treatment in the United States. These fertility brokers, who began offering "fertility holidays" in 2006, are important new actors at the center of reproductive travel.

Websites of IVF brokers must be considered "political economies of hope" (Rose and Novas 2005). Political economies of hope, which are propelled by organizations of infertile patients, extend the "hope" already embedded in reproductive technologies (Franklin 1997a). Brokers lure North Americans who desperately want a baby with the promise of white donors, a European vacation, and top-notch health care. Roughly two-thirds of the twenty-nine couples I met in the Czech Republic were pursuing IVF with an egg donor, rather than IVF with their own eggs. In addition, North Americans are seeking a European vacation alongside excellent health care. Doctors who care are painfully lacking in the United States' profit-hungry "baby business" (Spar 2006). Couples who choose to follow the path of reproductive travel make decisions based on complex notions of kinship, health care, and what constitutes a vacation. However, hope is the underlying basis of all of these factors.

Typically, North Americans traveling to the Czech Republic for in vitro fertilization are seeking gamete donation that will assure a biological connection with one parent and at least a physical resemblance to the other parent. We can distinguish these couples from those seeking children through international adoption from a country with children of markedly different ethnicity (Jacobson 2008). North Americans traveling to the Czech Republic are almost always seeking "white" babies from Czech egg or sperm donors (see also Kahn 2000:132; Nahman 2008). In using the term "white" I am referring to the dominant sociocultural logic of U.S. race and color lines. North Americans use the term "white" as if there is one variant of "white" (Rothman 2005:79). Racial categories label sets of physical characteristics that we can locate on the body (Rothman 2005:90). Notions of white have often been tied to ideas of purity, but in these cases whiteness is also tied closely to notions of relatedness.

This desire for "white" babies reflects an "appeal of European heritage" (Nash 2003:184). Scholars of international adoption to Russia and Eastern Europe have written about the ways that North Americans assume they can forge a deeper kinship connection through "sharing whiteness with a child" (Jacobson 2008:42). Jacobson further elaborates that whiteness is often assumed to be stable and passed through bloodlines (2008:63). North Americans traveling to the Czech Republic are trying to ensure racial stability for their families.

A Global Marketplace of Health Care

A global reproductive tourism industry indicates shifts in global policies of health care. Whittaker bears witness to "neoliberal readjustments of societies across the world to meet the demands of economic globalization" (2008:273). Countries across the globe have been shifting away from nationalized systems whereby the government assumes responsibility in providing universal health care to all citizens. Transitioning toward neoliberal health care models is often touted for its efficiency. The way patients make the decision to travel abroad for health care reflects a strengthening of the global, neoliberal model of consumer health care. In this model, patients essentially become consumers "choosing" from various possible treatment options. As consumers believe themselves to be free actors, they are simply choosing from various possible menu items. Responsibility has fallen on them as ostensibly free actors in a global medical marketplace.

As I traced North American fertility journeys halfway around the globe, I uncovered layers of contradiction embedded in global reproductive medicine. Scholars have already shown how reproductive technologies are "hope" technologies (Franklin 1997a) that both empower women, by offering new opportunities to try to have a baby, and disempower them, by pressuring women to continuously subject their bodies to these medical technologies with no end point in sight.

Medical anthropologists have often examined the power inherent in biomedicine, and feminist scholars note further the power embedded in reproductive medicine (Martin 1989; Rapp 2000; Davis-Floyd 2003). Many anthropologists have written about medicalization as disempowering to women, in that it assumes management over their bodies (Martin 1989; Turiel 1998). Even further, Sandelowski (1991) has written of how the promises of reproductive technologies often "compel" women to keep trying. However, even though reproductive medicine may in fact disempower some women, Sundby (2002) has insisted on the recognition of the empowering nature of reproductive technologies. Though these technologies tend to be distributed unevenly, they do offer couples a chance to conceive. Feminist theory has often failed to consider the actual experiences of women suffering infertility (Sandelowski 1990). This book explores the extent to which reproductive technologies remain complicated and even more ambiguous in a foreign setting.

This book focuses on the multiple contradictions that occur as reproductive travelers embrace an ideological vision of vacation proposed by brokers. These contradictions, largely embedded in the term "IVF holiday," point to the tensions and disjunctures of a global marketplace for health care. As consumers, these patients must make difficult decisions regarding their health, and medical tourism brokers have packaged fertility holidays to aid in their decision making. This volume argues that reproductive travel exacerbates the hope embedded in reproductive technologies, especially when they are marketed as holidays. It frames reproductive travel as a form of consumption motivated by complex layers of desire for white babies, a European vacation, better health care, and technological success. Each of these desires is further mired within its own contradictions. The volume demonstrates that reproductive tourists must be diligent consumers within a global neoliberal market of health care that perpetuates stratified reproduction.

Methods

I first heard of IVF Holiday in 2008, when a friend sent me a link to the company's website. I consider my initial foray into the world of reproductive travel somewhat akin to how most North Americans learn about it: through Google searches and word of mouth. This research is based on a multisited project conducted in North America and the Czech Republic between 2010 and 2012. It is the first in-depth ethnographic study of North American reproductive travel to the Czech Republic from the consumer's point of view. I gathered data through participant observation, surveys, focus groups, and interviews with the three primary social actors involved in the reproductive travel industry: North American reproductive travelers, Czech reproductive medicine providers, and brokers. Ethnographic research at two reproductive clinics in the Czech Republic, as well as with patient tourists after they returned from their travels, provides insight into their complex behaviors, motivations, and experiences of reproductive travel.

Anthropologists have discussed the logistical, ethical, and technical difficulties of gaining access to infertile couples, especially those who travel abroad seeking services (Inhorn 2004; Whittaker and Speier 2010). The anthropologist must rely on various intermediaries, depending on the circumstances. The two main brokers for the Czech Republic, IVF Holiday and IVF Choices, put me in contact with Czech clinics as well as former clients. Both brokers sent out a survey to past clients who had already traveled to the Czech Republic, which garnered thirty respondents. Many of these respondents agreed to a follow-up interview that took place during the fall of 2010.

During the summers of 2010 and 2011, I conducted participant observation at two Moravian clinics, as well as at sites of lodging for North Americans (see figure I.1). I also interviewed Czech coordinators and doctors and North American patient-travelers. The town of Zlín (pronounced Zleen) is small, with a population of 80,000, offering one or two family-owned accommodations, whereas Brno (pronounced BIR-no), the second-largest city in the Czech Republic, provides couples with various options, ranging from four-star hotels to apartment-like studios. North Americans in Brno are much more isolated from one another, un-

Figure I.1. The favorite pension.

like couples in Zlín, who often seek the comfort of other North Americans while abroad.

I conducted a total of thirty preliminary surveys with former reproductive travelers and fifty interviews: twenty-nine with reproductive travelers (seventeen with women only, eleven with couples together, and one with a man only), ten with fertility brokers, and eleven with Czech clinic personnel. Because infertility is often considered a woman's problem, and reproductive technologies are played out on women's bodies, it was primarily women who were the more vocal informants. Sometimes I interviewed only the woman, or, if I interviewed the couple together, the woman usually had more to say. I interviewed only one husband and wife separately. From December 2011 to September 2012, I traveled to Canada and thirteen different states within the United States to follow up with patients I had met in the Czech Republic. I conducted a total of nineteen follow-up life history interviews with North American patients and brokers. In total, I met twenty-nine couples. My informants have made fifty-one total trips to the Czech Republic, and twenty-eight children have been born.[3]

Overwhelmingly, couples were very positive and willing to speak to me. They were happy to have another American to speak English with, particularly one who asked about their struggles. In the Czech Republic, I conducted interviews outside the North American–favored pension, in cafés and restaurants, in my room or their room, in the main lobby, at the local mall, or at the clinic (see figures I.2 and I.3). I shared many meals with American couples: breakfasts in the lobby of the pension or outside if the weather permitted and dinners at local favorite restaurants. I went to the town center, the local museum, the observation tower, and even the zoo, joining couples on their small excursions around town.

During my final phase of research in North America, I met some couples at their favorite local restaurants in their hometowns, while others invited me into their homes. I shared cappuccinos or Little Caesar's pizza and sweet tea with them. I maintain electronic communication with most, through either social media or e-mail. They keep me updated with news of their burgeoning families. Of course, I was not able to follow up with every couple that I met. Often those who suffer the pain of a failed cycle retreat to heal. As Throsby has shown in her study of failed cycles, "Those whose treatment fails literally drop out of the sight of the treatment providers" (2004:7).

Figure I.2 The clinic waiting room.

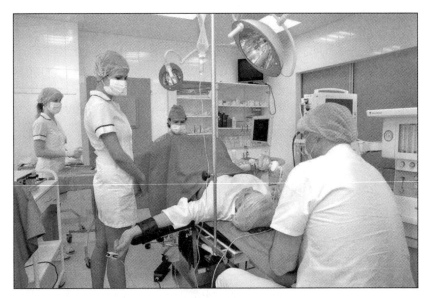

Figure I.3 The operating room of the clinic.

Fertility Vacationers

Those traveling to the Czech Republic for fertility treatment are predominantly white, lower-class to middle-class North Americans. Two Canadian women are included in this research because gamete donors cannot be paid in Canada (which makes it difficult for those who need an egg donor to find one). Canadians who can afford treatment in the United States will generally travel south for treatment. However, those who cannot afford treatment in the United States will also travel to the Czech Republic. I encountered women whose husbands worked three jobs to provide for the entire family, working-class couples, and upper-middle-class couples and women. The majority of reproductive travelers I met were from the lower middle class.[4] The reproductive traveler is careful with her "fertility dollar," a savvy consumer.

Typically, North American reproductive travelers are in their late thirties or early forties, since the majority need IVF with an egg donor. Of thirty survey respondents, the average age was 40.3, with ages ranging from 27 to 53. They are from all over North America, including Florida, Georgia, South Carolina, Tennessee, Indiana, Illinois, Nebraska, Wisconsin, Minnesota, California, Washington, and Texas. My respondents are mainly white, although I did interview one Puerto Rican couple and one African American couple. The majority of travelers are experienced in the world of ARTs, having undergone several IUIs in the United States, often with the help of fertility drugs. They may have even tried one or more IVF cycles before reaching the limits of their budget. North American reproductive tourists are relatively well traveled, although several were venturing abroad for the first time.

Tracing Fertility Journeys

This book traces North American fertility journeys, which can be considered a form of biological citizenship (Rose and Novas 2005). Rose claims that "conceptions of 'biological citizenship' have taken shape that recode the duties, rights, and expectations of human beings in relation to their sickness, and also to their life itself, reorganize the relations between individuals and their biomedical authorities, and reshape the ways in which human beings relate to themselves as 'somatic individuals'" (2007:6). Petryna, who uses the label "biological citizenship" to capture collective and individual social practices of Ukrainians demanding social welfare within a democratizing, post-Soviet post-Chernobyl nation-state, considers the complex ways citizens "use biology, scientific knowledge and suffering to have access to cultural resources" under harsh market transitions (2003:3). Rose builds on this by noting that biological citizenship can take many forms (2007:25). One form is the patient support networks that develop online and abroad. While North Americans are not undergoing a harsh transition to a market economy, nor are they demanding social welfare; they are assuming responsibility for managing their own bodies and also assuming risk when they venture abroad for treatment.

The book's first chapter introduces North Americans who have been diagnosed with infertility and describes their reactions and the culturally meaningful ways they respond. Often, their responses are contradictory. There are particular stages of treatment using reproductive technologies, and this chapter traces these patients' movement through the "baby business" in the United States (Spar 2006). Ultimately, the chapter ends with their alienation and disillusionment with overpriced treatment options.

Chapter 2 follows North Americans who turn to various forms of social media as a way of learning about possible routes toward parenthood. It is on the Internet that they learn of reproductive travel to the Czech Republic and become diligent consumers conducting research. This chapter follows female patients as they enter virtual biosocial communities where they join online gendered support groups and engage in biomedical global citizenship. With the North American patients, we encounter IVF brokers who are packaging fertility holidays that promise a stress-free IVF cycle in a relaxing European setting. The marketing of fertility holidays online speaks to North American hopes, both for a child who resembles them and for the liberating aspects of travel (Löfgren 1999).

In chapter 3 we witness the global encounters between North American patients and Czech doctors. The chapter uncovers the shifting role of the Czech clinics as they provide patient-centered care. I frame the entire industry as a global care route and trace global technologies, finance, images, and people enmeshed in "intimate labor" (Boris and Parreñas 2010). Czech fertility clinics are global checkout lanes for North American global biocitizens opting to purchase IVF with egg donation. Yet the economic nature of these transactions is minimized by affective discourse.

The book continues in chapter 4 with a consideration of the social kinship bonds that are created and sustained at the local pension. At the same time, I deconstruct the fundamental contradictions embedded within "fertility holidays." Women internalize the pressure to "relax" and treat their trip as a vacation in the hope of ensuring a successful pregnancy.

Finally, chapter 5 follows North Americans as they return home, with or without a successful pregnancy. It traces the new difficulties many have with complicated pregnancies and raising multiples, and the sorrow of those who are not successful. It continues with an analysis of social kinship as it is sustained by women's kin work via social media (di Leonardo 1987; Pande 2015). Essentially, social kinship networks of families with children born of egg donation in the Czech Republic continue to expand into new kinds of relationships. In addition, a majority of the couples engage in return reproductive travel to the Czech Republic for multiple cycles of IVF.

The book concludes with suggestions for future avenues of research, even as I argue for stricter regulations of the baby business. Furthermore, it offers an explanation about how North American reproductive travel is both particular and global. While North Americans' reactions to infertility and blocked access to treatment based on cost are culturally specific, their journeys also reflect a global trend toward privatized health care.

1

From Hope to Alienation

North Americans Enter the Baby Business

There are a lot of people out there that can't afford it . . . better than half the country. It is still out of their price range for that kind of money. You know as long as they've got 45,000 people that are getting it done and paying them $15,000 to $30,000, they're going to keep charging them. . . . If money dictates whether you can conceive or not, or you spend so much money to conceive that now the kid's born and you lose your house because you've got nothing left. That's problematic.
—Tom, IVF broker

Undoubtedly, parenthood remains a norm in our society (Throsby 2004:16). The couples with whom I spoke faced multiple layers of suffering, which included depression, bodily betrayal, social isolation, and stigma. They propelled themselves through the baby business armed with American cultural notions about health and hope. In fact, the market of infertility medicine produces and depends on this "hope."

Infertile couples try to think "positively," a cultural script they use to deal with the emotional toll of treatment. However, conflicting ideas about hard work and luck, or "stress" and positive thinking, incur more contradictions that have already been shown to be inherent in the world of ARTs. Assisted reproductive technologies exacerbate the extent to which "women feel compelled by their doctors and male partners to undergo medical treatments for infertility because of the strong cultural pressure for married couples to have children and to demonstrate their normality in reproducing" (Sandelowski 1991:33).

Patients I met embody the typical "compulsion to try" numerous cycles of treatment, as they are encouraged to never give up, to work hard, and to think positively. Yet as they move deeper into the baby business of North America, many become increasingly angered and disillusioned by what they interpret to be doctors' greed and lack of care. They are critical of the process and feel as if they are being treated like a wallet or a number.[1] The baby business of North America appears to them to have forgotten about the importance of providing care.

Becker's classic study (2000) has revealed the ways in which global forces of consumer culture have influenced the growth of the reproductive medical industry in North America. Her work also elucidates North American patient responses to the dizzying array of medical options, showing how their responses reflect notions of biology, gender, and the body. My study uncovered similar experiences for infertile couples, but my focus is distinct in revealing the neoliberal ideology that permeates North American responses to infertility. As described by Horton and colleagues, "In advanced liberal societies, the notion of individual responsibility for health has become enmeshed with the idea of responsible citizenship, as prudent individuals voluntarily purchase health insurance plans and undertake preventative health checks, genetic testing, and lifestyle changes" (2014:3). Indeed, in the United States, "the right to health has been reconfigured as a right to consumer choice—in terms of health insurance plans, physicians, and pharmaceuticals" (3). Nikolas Rose identifies a general shift away from the governmental responsibility for the management of health as devolving to "quasi-autonomous regulatory bodies—bioethics commissions, for example; to private corporations—like private fertility clinics . . . to professional groups" (2007:3). In addition, patients must increasingly maneuver among these various private groups when managing their health.

Becker (2000) has described the commercial market for reproductive medicine in North America and the difficult decisions couples confront. She shows how access to reproductive medicine is a class and gendered phenomenon, as profit motives and medical care coalesce. Throsby (2004) has convincingly shown the centrality of women's bodies and identities to the meaning and practice of IVF. In this chapter, I connect North American cultural responses to infertility with a medical model of individual responsibility for one's health, which is rapidly escalating under neoliberal market conditions. Clarke and colleagues regard health within our biomedical system as "an ongoing moral self-transformation . . . something to work toward" (2003:172). Ultimately, infertile women are self-disciplining their bodies and their functions outside of the comprehensive care of a provider (Clarke et al. 2003:172). New patterns of patient behavior have developed in which individual responsibility for one's own health is promoted and sustained. This is a central piece of the neoliberal model of health care.

When couples confront infertility, they often respond by embracing ideological notions of hard work in pursuing IVF within the United States (Franklin 1997a). Contradictions are embedded in cultural responses to infertility, as couples attempt to work hard while they gamble with reproductive technologies and try to embody good mental and physical health.

Couples Confront Infertility

The American Society for Reproductive Medicine estimates that infertility affects 6.1 million North American women; roughly one in eight couples of reproductive age experiences this inability to "make babies" (C. Thompson 2005:7). In narrating their infertility journeys, couples I met mentioned a point in their lives when their friends began having children, which can be understood as a social cue for the "normal" or right time to start a family. In the summer of 2011, I met Janice and Craig, who were in their early forties. Their tans from living in the Sunshine State gleamed under the streetlight when I first met them, sitting outside of the pension in Zlín across from Lauren and John. The two blonds, Janice and Craig, were both nurses and had met at work. They had been married for ten years, and they usually spent their summers in her home country, Canada, something I gleaned from Janice's subtle accent. They were planning on building their own house on a piece of land they had already purchased in central Florida. Craig remembers, "[At] about thirty-five, maybe seven years ago, we had a large group of friends, all about the same age, you know, midthirties. We're all teachers and nurses, and we all hung out. Then everybody started deciding to have children, and we just kept trying." It took two years of trying, with one year of "timed" intercourse, before they realized something was wrong.

Since the advent of the birth control pill, North Americans have held onto the notion that they can prevent conception when they do not want it, but also can easily initiate it when they do. Unfortunately, contraception and conception are not the same things (Greil and McQuillan 2010). Over breakfast I met a very chatty couple from Los Angeles, Maureen and Daniel. I had seen many of Maureen's postings on a website for women thinking about traveling to the Czech Republic, so I had anticipated their arrival, always eager to meet more people. Daniel described how they met at a community college in San Diego, where they realized they shared many of the same interests in film and editing. They carried a newly purchased iPad with them everywhere, pulling up Czech phrases, maps, and pictures of their travels. I could tell they were technologically savvy. They had been together for fifteen years and married for six. Daniel commented dryly that once they started trying to have children, on the heels of many of their friends, "A strange perception from a guy is that you spend most of your life hoping you don't get pregnant. I'm sure women are the same way, but the guys really worry about it. It's a big worry. Then all of a sudden, it's like, God, it's so much harder than you're taught in school." When conception does not happen immediately, North American couples often grow impatient and frustrated, assuming it should happen easily, the "natural" way (Becker 2000:7).

The Universal Declaration of Human Rights, Article 16, claims, "Men and women of full age, without any limitation due to race, nationality or religion, have the right to marry and to found a family. They are entitled to equal rights as to marriage, during marriage and at its dissolution" (United Nations 2015). The discourse of "rights" is prevalent when people speak of infertility, which is understood as hindering one's right to have a child or start a family. Rothman links this discourse of rights to capitalism: "Women, like men, lay claim to their own bodies and to their own children and call on the basic values of capitalism to support those claims" (2006:21). She mentions our notions of the body as something that is "viewed not as a resource for the community or the society, but as private property, a personal resource" (21). The discourse on one's right to have a family becomes a talking point for those who suffer infertility.

Infertility interrupts normative ideas of one's life stages. However, the point at which North Americans begin to think about having children has shifted over the past few decades, reflecting cultural trends of women in higher education and the workforce and in divorce rates. "The timing of parenthood has changed," and the delay of childbearing has complex effects (Becker 2000:37). In North America, there is a general trend of women seeking higher education and careers before getting married, and North Americans, on average, have children at twenty-four to twenty-six years of age (Kottak 2011:139, 141). The decline in marriage rates, along with high divorce rates combined with remarriage, can be credited with a drop in heterosexual reproduction (Stone 2014:240–248). After putting off marriage and childbearing, or marrying a second or third time, people are often shocked when they find that being older can hinder their ability to conceive. It "wreaks havoc on life plans" (Becker 2000:37). In addition to age-related infertility, there are other causes of infertility: roughly 30 percent of cases are male factor infertility, where men may have a low sperm count or low sperm motility. Another 30 percent of cases are female factor, where a woman's tubes may be blocked or scarred from endometriosis or prior pelvic infection. In the other 40 percent of cases, infertility remains unexplained. However, the ways in which North Americans confront this knowledge reflect cultural notions about health.

Despite the fact that infertility can be either female or male factor, it has been well documented that dealing with infertility is a largely gendered phenomenon. According to Park, "Women appear to be more stigmatized for their childlessness than do their male counterparts" (2002:26). Women are the ones who must assume the "work" of pursuing medical treatment through reproductive technologies, and they "bear the burden of medical intervention" (Throsby 2004:18). Given the stigma of infertility, many keep their problem a secret or pursue treatment secretly (see also Nahar and van der Geest 2014:381). Furthermore, Rose identifies the individual moral responsibility for one's health and one's family's health as the social obligation of women (2007:29).

Women I interviewed, in wondering why they are unable to conceive, often say defensively or perplexedly that they are healthy. They see themselves as following the medical model of how to get pregnant: they must first get healthy. They have been upstanding citizens who practice yoga, eat well, and take care of themselves, reinscribing the ideology that health is an individual responsibility. However, this ideology then leads to women feeling cheated by their bodies when they do not conceive easily. I met Claudia and Ben, a couple from Seattle, over my first breakfast at the pension in the summer of 2011. They were very calm and relaxed, having already spent more than a week in the Czech Republic. I was catching up with them on their second-to-last morning in Zlín. They are both very tall, fit, and health-conscious, maintaining a vegetarian diet—which I could tell when they left the delicious bacon untouched. When I interviewed the two of them later that afternoon in their third-floor apartment, Claudia exuded an air of calm, having just meditated and written in her journal. She repeatedly stated that she is a healthy person, which made it difficult for her to understand her infertility: "I have no idea, because I'm a very healthy person. I never thought I'd have a problem having a child, and it's been unexplained. I've had every test, every whatever. I have a perfectly normal cycle. I always have, but this is all unexplained."

In addition to this confusion about their infertility, some women wondered aloud why friends whom they considered unhealthy still were able to conceive. I met Valerie at the clinic during my second week in the summer of 2010. She pushed her long, dark hair behind her ears as she leaned in and spoke loudly over the quiet clinic sounds. She carried a stack of papers that included her medical history, as her husband, Dan, shrank into a corner holding tightly onto a tour book of Vienna. The two were from San Diego and had met when Valerie was in her late thirties. During our interview the next day outside of the pension, she remembered that they were both surprised when she accidentally became pregnant early in their relationship. They decided to get married, only to suffer successive miscarriages. In her anger and frustration, she lamented: "I had one girlfriend who's forty-two years old, overweight, eats like crap, and she got pregnant and had a baby, damn it. Why can't I? I'm healthier than her. You know?" There is a moral dimension that tinges the way many women speak of a person's health, as if only the woman who assumes responsibility for a healthy diet and sensible weight deserves to get pregnant. The women in my sample recounted how, when they attempted to get pregnant, they had eliminated alcohol and caffeine from their diet or done other things to attain a healthy status. Many women not only feel morally compelled to assume self-care but also feel "morally obliged to avail [themselves] of new biotechnological resources" (Guell 2012:519). Thus, when confronted with infertility, they often turn to reproductive technologies.

The owner of one of the IVF broker companies, Petra, is a slim, stunning Czech woman with ash-blonde hair carelessly pulled into a ponytail, defining her high cheekbones as her blue eyes twinkle. I had contacted Petra over the phone and arranged to meet her in the early summer of 2010. She invited me to have an "American" breakfast in her sprawling suburban Atlanta home the first time I met her. Over crispy bacon and fried eggs, she told me about her personal experience as a woman who suffers infertility. She told me how she and her husband, though they married after dating for only four months, had waited until they were financially stable before trying to have children. Like most others, she thought she would get pregnant immediately. Petra remembers trying to conceive: "At some point I was so stressed, so obsessed, I mean, we were timing the intercourse to the minute. I was constantly talking about it. I was envious of those that told me they were pregnant. I mean, the whole shebam [sic]. I mean, it's just a part of infertility."

Petra speaks quickly, bluntly, and to the point. She is petite, and a powerhouse of energy. Petra claimed that some women, like her, are simply "stress control freaks" who can't get pregnant because of their personalities. High levels of stress indicate the intense level of emotional investment women experience during this process. Petra complained, "Nobody told me that you might prevent it [conception] from actually happening just because you're so stressed out." The management of one's stress can be considered an element of this individual control over one's health. Thus, women not only are responsible for their physical health but also must monitor their mental health. A myth that circulates throughout conversations about getting pregnant (one that hinges on a woman's ability or inability to contain her stress) is the idea that if you "relax," you will get pregnant. Stories abound of couples who proceed with adoption, only to then find themselves pregnant.

In addition to the stress of infertility, women may suffer from depression. Craig, the nurse from Florida, described the emotional journey of infertility: "I will say one thing. Having been in the infertility thing and having so many years of disappointments, when you first start every month, it's a disappointment, and then every procedure's a disappointment. You prepare yourself, like right now, transfer is tomorrow and you're all having fun, but you have these depressing moments. It's like 50 percent, [I'm] prepared for the worst. I think too, I think my wife's very positive." This need for positive thinking amid stress, fear, and depression becomes another moral axiom and ties into the ideology of hope, particularly for women.

Stigmatized Childlessness

Becker examines the stigma associated with infertility as cultural and bodily, building on Irving Goffman's classic sociological analysis of stigma as "an undesired differentness from what we had anticipated" (1963:5). Becker highlights infertility as a bodily stigma because it "belies abnormality" for the couple (2000:45). In addition to this stigma of infertility, couples I interviewed found their stigma to be compounded by indifferent treatment from doctors. For example, North American couples undergoing IVF must often undergo psychological testing, which entails going over alternative forms of family planning and promoting relaxation to help them prepare for a possible negative outcome. The promotion of relaxation techniques also plays into the myth that relaxing aids in conception. Some clinics require these procedures in order to protect themselves against possible future litigation.

In the early summer of 2011, I met a woman who was at the pension alone for a large part of her stay. She and I became fast friends, sharing breakfast daily and going for long hikes to fill the quiet summer days. Alison spent many nights Skyping with her family back in Minnesota, and I could tell how excited she was when her husband's visit drew near. Alison and Andy were high school sweethearts who had decided to wait to have children until they were thirty. After a year of trying to conceive with no results, they learned Andy's sperm count was extremely low. They had a failed IVF cycle in Minnesota, in which no embryos had been fertilized in vitro. According to the nurse at the clinic, this occurrence was a complete fluke. Alison was, of course, very frustrated. She wanted to undergo another cycle, but her doctor told her she needed another psychological assessment before continuing. Alison remembers reaching her limit:

> Then [the doctor] made the nurse come in and say, "Oh you guys need to go through therapy again." We already did it once, and we had to do

it through their clinic. I had had it at that point, because I've already done it. Does everyone have to? Not only that, but no one else has to go through that to have a baby. Why do I? Why am I different? If I made this decision, it should be between myself, my husband, and our God. If we felt that we needed to go to a therapist, we would go to our own. So that was the end of that.

At that point, Alison was done seeking treatment in the United States. She also became irritated if she felt that her friends or family were pussyfooting around the topic of pregnancy, as if she were overly fragile. Her defenses were up against the label of being "too sensitive."

Some women choose not to tell others about their attempts at getting pregnant, since they want to avoid any potential judgment that they are "desperate." While Claudia and Ben felt that their friends were nothing but supportive, Claudia did worry that they would think she and Ben were trying "too hard." It is often deemed "natural" that a woman desperately wants a child, but "it is also possible for that desire to be deemed dangerously out of control" (Throsby 2004:4). Women must walk a fine line between monitoring their mental and physical health, stress, and working hard to conceive yet not "too hard."

Those facing infertility experience an additional layer of suffering from the stigma of leading childless lives. Because there is no cultural script for conversations with friends who are suffering infertility, the average person is often at a loss for words (Layne 2003). Couples I met reported that they felt a lack of empathy or understanding from friends and family, and consequently experienced a sense of isolation with their infertility. As we caught up in the summer of 2012 over dinner in Memphis, April told me how she was frustrated at the statements she often heard from her friends, who in their attempts to show empathy sometimes struck a wrong nerve. Over barbeque nachos, we shared common clichés people offer. The one that struck her was: "'It isn't in God's time,' and it's like, OK, I know you don't have anything else to say, but I don't want to hear that. I know they don't know what to say." Generally speaking, women dealing with infertility suffer depression, stress, and stigma. All the while, the promises suggested by possibilities of ARTs lure them again and again to keep trying (Franklin 1997b).

Never Giving Up

Louise Brown was the first baby born via in vitro fertilization, in 1978 in the United Kingdom, an event that was covered extensively by the media. In 1981, the first U.S. IVF baby was born. Since these first successful cycles using ARTs, debates have raged concerning the medicalization of reproduction. Many discussions surrounding ARTs center on the question of what is "natural" when it comes to conception. Over the past twenty-five years, the line of what is considered "natural" reproduction has repeatedly shifted as infertile couples continue to demand access to ARTs. In fact, the progressive march of technological advances in reproductive medicine is fueled by consumer demand.[2]

Once a couple's infertility has been confirmed, there is a general progression of stages in assisted reproductive treatment. At each stage, a couple may feel as if a successful pregnancy is just around the corner. First, as we witnessed in April's case, described in the introduction, a woman takes drugs that will stimulate her ovaries to produce more than one egg. Once a woman has started taking medication, she will continue to have "timed relations." The next step is intrauterine sperm injection, which is essentially using a catheter to place a number of sperm directly into the uterus. Some couples I met did only one or a few cycles of IUI, like April and Larry. But others I met did upwards of a dozen. For couples who meet later in life, attempts at IUIs may seem to be only "shooting in the dark." As Sarah Franklin found in her work, "A major component of the experience of IVF is the accumulation of an increasing amount of information about the technical complexity of conception" (1997b:104).

Claudia and Ben had both been married before, so Claudia already knew that she had fertility issues when they first met passing one another on a street in Seattle. They had tried to get pregnant nearly from the beginning of their relationship. Once they began medical treatment, they did five rounds of IUI, at which point they saw IVF as the "next step." Once a couple has attempted several cycles of IUI, they reach a point when they are encouraged to try IVF. Although medical protocols vary when it comes to IVF, women take birth control pills so they are able to time the moment of ovulation. In addition, a woman continues taking medication to stimulate her ovaries to produce more than one follicle, self-administering daily shots into her lower abdomen. Right before a woman ovulates, her eggs are retrieved and mixed with sperm. The resulting embryos are given a three- or five-day blastocyst period to "grow" while in vitro.[3] Next, a doctor transfers chosen embryos directly into a woman's uterine lining, where it is hoped that they will attach.

If the cause of infertility is age-related, a woman may be encouraged to try IVF using eggs of a younger donor, which increases the chance of a successful cycle. Although men have been donating sperm for a long time, the introduction of egg donors into rounds of IVF has increased the debate surrounding the ethical dimensions of reproductive technologies. While both sperm and egg donation introduce a third party into the reproductive equation, Almeling (2007) has shown how cultural notions of motherhood and fatherhood influence different attitudes toward sperm and egg donation. In vitro fertilization allows for a split between biological, gestational, and social mother, introducing new questions of "parenthood" (Ragoné 2005). Women who cannot carry a baby to term may be encouraged to use a surrogate, who will go through the IVF cycle. For each progressive stage of infertility treatment in the United States, the price tag continues to climb.[4] It may take several years for a couple to move through these stages, and they may still emerge childless.

Feminist scholars have illustrated the contradictory nature of reproductive technologies (Sundby 2002; Sandelowski 1990, 1991). On the one hand, women who had trouble conceiving before now have a better chance to conceive with ARTs. On the other side of the equation, scholars have revealed the "compulsive" nature of reproductive technologies, whereby women feel compelled to keep submitting their bodies to these "hope" technologies. Couples have "an equally strong desire to feel that every possible option has been pursued in the attempt to have a child" (Franklin 1997b:107). Inspirational quotes on posters in offices throughout North America urge people to be themselves, to be different, to not let anything get in the way of expressing their individuality. These words promoting individualism are meant to inspire, to instill hope. A compelling force, Becker explains, "Hope is closely associated with American notions of individualism and responsibility for health, and it has become embedded within the process of commodification of reproductive medicine" (2000:117; see also Clarke et al. 2003:162). At the same time, North

American individuality is defined via consumption—in the clothes that are worn, the cars that are driven, and the homes that are purchased (Rothman 2005:36). This unchecked celebration of the individual is the other side of the coin of the brave, independent individuals who must assume responsibility for their health and life paths. Scholars have written about the ways in which "health is seen to be the responsibility of the individuals" (Whyte, van der Geest, and Hardon 2003:50; see also Rosenfeld and Faircloth 2006:5).

In the fall of 2013, the story of Diana Nyad's successful swim from Cuba to Florida was celebrated. At the time, I noticed her messages of hope being posted on social media sites and on news outlets. Her message had three points: essentially, to never give up, to never stop chasing your dreams, and that swimming is a team sport. Her first two ideas are congruent with how North Americans often approach the world of ARTs. As new medical advances are made, couples inevitably feel "compelled to try" any way possible to have a baby, using terms of persistence and not giving up (Sandelowski 1991). Women find themselves continually trying new procedures to get pregnant (Becker 2000; Sandelowski 1991; Franklin 1997b). In fact, the American Society for Reproductive Medicine has raised concerns about the exploitation of infertility patients by profit-driven clinicians (Becker 2000).

In addition to a woman's responsibility to maintain her health and avoid stress, there is another moral axiom for women to "not give up." Women often feel like failures if they give up. As described by Throsby, "Within this discourse, 'giving up' is a personal moral failure to fight the good fight—in this case, to continue to work towards pregnancy" (2004:15). The ideology and also the hard work of positive thinking (Ehrenreich 2009) in North American culture pervade discourse about fertility treatment. Patients often remember a close friend or family member urging them to not "give up," as if giving up was immoral, because perseverance and "hard work" would inevitably pay off. I happened to be sitting in the foyer of the pension one afternoon, and I met Chris as he was coming in armed with smoothies for himself and his wife, Angela, who was resting after her egg transfer. I interviewed them later that evening after they returned from dinner. Angela's father had been a professor, so she empathized with my need for interviewees. She and Chris were from Chicago, and they had recently tried to adopt, but it had fallen through. Angela was forty-seven, Chris was fifty-one, and they had met six years earlier. Given Angela's age, they had begun trying to conceive immediately after getting married. After relaying her fertility journey of many IUIs and a cycle of IVF, she joked, "That's how quickly you become forty-seven." After their adoption had fallen apart, one of Angela's friends had gotten pregnant at a famous clinic in Colorado. She remembers her friend urging her to try *one more* IVF cycle, saying she didn't want to see her "give up." Her friend acknowledged that she knew the hell Angela and Chris had gone through, but she still pushed them to try one more time.

Couples spoke of not wanting to look back and wonder, "What if?" We see how their social support system reinforces the moral axiom of positive thinking, as friends or family members believe they can encourage by urging the sufferer to keep fighting and working hard, further perpetuating the stigma of childlessness. In this sense, undergoing further cycles of in vitro fertilization becomes a moral necessity. If one cycle of IVF does not work, doctors will change the protocol and encourage the couple to try another cycle. There is the sense that they need to play one more hand.

Gambling Compulsions

I did three IVFs and then two frozen transfers, and, like I said, at that point, it was $90,000 and I was done. And I couldn't be done. I just, I mean, it's addictive or something. I don't know.

—Abby, single patient

Patients I interviewed often told me of their endless attempts to get pregnant, which signaled this compulsive side of reproductive medicine. I met Jenny in the small Moravian town of Zlín in the summer of 2011. She and her husband were from the West Coast. Their toddler twins had been conceived via IVF using egg donation at the local clinic a few years before, and they were returning to try for a sibling. Jenny was a petite, highly energetic woman, who had to keep up with their twins—a feat I could barely do for an hour when I babysat them during her embryo transfer. She spoke rapidly and dramatically about her early history with

ARTs as we chatted at the clinic while she rested after her transfer, and after I had with relief handed the children back to her husband:

> They started me on all kinds of drugs. I would say I probably broke the limit to how many times they give you Clomid, and then how many times they give you injectable. I would probably say I did at least thirty cycles, medicated cycles, which is totally way over the limit. And toward the end they got nothing but the usual monthly egg. And so finally they did IUI. I even forgot what it was called, it's been so long. The first one worked, and then it was like it lasted like a week, so it was like a chemical thing,[5] and of course it gives you false hope. So I think they did a total of, and this is a ballpark figure because I lost track, but I want to say fifteen IUIs. That's quite a few. So I've actually probably had the most experience [of my sample].

She said this somewhat proudly, as if to demonstrate her resolve and determination.

It was apparent in talking to certain women that they felt compelled to keep trying. Petra, the energetic IVF broker, had gone through an extreme number of IVF cycles. When I first met her in 2010 and asked her the number, she sighed heavily and recounted: "OK, let's see . . . two frozen,[6] fresh, frozen, fresh, frozen, fresh, frozen, fresh, I had four fresh cycles, four frozen ones, and a fifth frozen one that was for the surrogate." My mind boggled; it was easy to lose count. She recalled, "September 2006 was my first IVF, and the surrogate was October 2008, so yeah, two years exactly. Back to back to back. I think I gave my body maybe a month or two to rest between." When I completed my final interview with Petra in 2012, she had had a total of eleven cycles and had successfully given birth to her own child after having had a daughter via surrogate a few years earlier.

Given the excessive number of cycles some women undergo, many used a "lay logic" (Knoll 2001) of gambling: the more times you try, the more your chances increase. Unfortunately, the same probability happens each cycle, just as it does every time you roll the dice. Yet most people are unfamiliar with concepts of probability (Chibnik 2011:18). One's chances do not increase with the number of attempts. North American discourse consisted of talking about the "odds" via success rates, or "taking a chance" on IVF. When clinics publish success rates in percentages, and speak to couples using pie charts, the rates become part of the decision-making process of whether or not they will pursue further treatment. However, it is difficult to make choices about health care where success rates are only 20 percent (Mol 2008). As in the case of "paid volunteers" who act as "professional guinea pigs" for pharmaceutical companies, there is "a cultural context in which individuals make decisions about risks and benefits" (Abadie 2010:19). This risk taking, again, is an individual patient's undertaking, reinforcing a neoliberal model of individual responsibility for health (and risk). Lupton (1999) has written about the ways that a pregnant woman must assume responsibility for her unborn child by managing and weighing potential risks. Of course, this management of risk also falls onto the shoulders of women trying to get pregnant using ARTs.

Cindy, aged forty-two, and Scott, thirty-one, lived in Montana. They were the last couple I happened to meet at the clinic, just as I was taking leave and thanking the nurses for their time. After taking Cindy and Scott to a favorite nearby restaurant for their first night in Zlín, I interviewed them in their spacious, orange-hued apartment at the pension. Scott had been in the military and worked in construction. They had not had any "luck" with several rounds of IUI. Cindy referred to a woman's egg reserve as a gumball machine that contained green (good) eggs, yellow (OK) eggs, and red (bad) eggs near the end of a woman's fertility. She continued, "So then, so by my age, I have very few green gumballs left. But, I mean, it's possible, 'cause there's many women that can still have their own, but I didn't have any luck at all." She knew that IVF with her own eggs gave her only a 5 percent chance of success, which she wasn't willing to gamble on because it would have cost $12,000. Individuals who are weighing options for conception via reproductive technologies must consider risks on their own as patient-consumers in a neoliberal marketplace of health care.

Nickel-and-Dimed

Here I think it's more about the almighty dollar. We checked out in vitro here. It started out at $10,000, not including medication, and then they tack this on and they tack that on, and, well, ICSI is this, and retrieving your eggs is this. I mean, that was a big surprise. And by the time they got done tacking everything on, it was over $30,000 for less than 30 percent chance.

—Maria, patient

North American demand for IVF has remained "constant," yet the price acts as a severe constraint for lower-class and middle-class North Americans. Debora Spar has characterized the U.S. fertility trade as a "baby business," since it is a largely unregulated, for-profit endeavor. Due to the high profit and endless demand for services, North American clinics have little incentive to reduce their prices. Thus, the North American fertility market is "punctuated by inequities," whereby only those who can afford treatment can access it (Spar 2006:96). The "selection of who receives treatment is driven by a private medicalized market in which only a few select individuals can afford treatment; thus medicalized infertility may be medicalized only for some" (Bell 2009:692). According to Throsby, "In the US, it is estimated that two-thirds of couples experiencing infertility do not seek treatment" (2004:6).

Reproductive medicine has been complicit with the commodification of health care. Clarke et al. describe reproductive medicine in the United States as an "out of pocket boutique," with varying medical options (2003:171). Reproductive medicine typifies a neoliberal, consumer model of privatized health care. To consumers of reproductive medicine, "the coalescence of business and medicine is . . . obvious" (Becker 2000:245). Couples who enter the world of fertility medicine quickly become aware that the clinic is, in fact, a business. Kimbrell has referred to this business as "the human body shop" where gametes are sold, and he argues that reproductive medicine "represents the invasion of the market into our most intimate selves" (1993:73). Kimbrell's association of IVF with commodification denies any benefits that may result from reproductive technologies. But, in fact, most middle-class and upper-class couples who face infertility will turn to medical solutions if they are available (C. Thompson 2005:3).

When I began this research project, the IVF brokers put me in contact with some of their past clients. Faith was a client who had created a website that was meant to provide North Americans with information specifically about a clinic in the town of Zlín. She had been one of the clinic's early foreign clients, who had had a daughter from her first cycle of IVF. I initially talked to Faith by phone in the fall of 2010 and finally met her in her home in Georgia in December 2011. Faith and her husband, Michael, had been married for two months when she first got pregnant, yet she miscarried at six weeks. She was pregnant again four months later, yet miscarried at five weeks. After a year, Faith visited her doctor—who sent her on her way, saying that because she'd gotten pregnant twice, she was fine. She and her husband kept trying, but there were no more pregnancies after two years of marriage. She went back to her doctor, who gave her Clomid, a synthetic estrogen, after declaring Faith and Michael "normal" after a series of diagnostic tests with no results that explained the miscarriages. Faith did eight rounds of Clomid, then four with letrozole, and then four IUIs. It was only at this point that she and Michael discovered they had two problems: she had polycystic ovarian syndrome, and her husband had a low sperm count. It had taken two and a half years to reach this diagnosis.

Once the doctor at a clinic in Atlanta diagnosed their problems, he told them they would need IVF to have children. Faith had really liked her doctor at the clinic, finding him personable and caring. Yet when that doctor left, the clinic began to feel cold and became just a business. "Sometimes," she explained, "I felt like a cow in a herd, just being processed." Then Faith began to wonder why their diagnosis had taken so long, thinking that the clinic had dragged things out. She thought the clinicians should have realized there was a problem after the first failed IUI, but instead they encouraged the couple to do three more injections, which cost a total of $10,000.

Faith and Michael are not rich; he is a paramedic and a firefighter, and she was a secretary at the time. She emphasized that they were not making a high income. When the doctor suggested IVF and said it would cost another $16,000 (which was at a 10 percent discounted rate), their hearts sank. In addition to the baseline price, the other fees for freezing leftover embryos, the ICSI procedure, and a five-day blastocyst amounted to $26,000 for one round of IVF. Faith was astounded by this price tag for a procedure that the clinic said had only an estimated 20 percent success rate. In addition, the doctor told them that he would only transfer one embryo, or possibly two if the second one had a low grade. Faith thought with exasperation about how hard her husband was working at his three jobs just to try for one child. They were pouring all of their money into an iffy treatment, one for which they had no insurance coverage.

The high cost of IVF is compounded by the lack of insurance coverage, which my survey respondents found frustrating. The Affordable Care Act that became effective in January 2014, as I was writing this chapter, does not mandate that fertility treatment be covered. Currently, fifteen of the fifty states mandate at least some type of infertility treatment, but this rarely covers IVF with an egg donor. For women I met, some procedures were covered, such as surgeries to battle endometriosis. However, these procedures constituted only about 20 percent of the total cost of roughly $10,000 for one cycle. Daniel, who worked in the film industry in Southern California, had insurance, yet he admitted, "We knew that there was no way we could get any kind of coverage through the insurance company, which is altogether a very strange circumstance, because it seems like most insurance companies don't even want to cover [IVF] at all. It seems like a very strange thing to not want to cover, you know? Insurance companies don't want you to have children."

Even more, a couple suffering infertility may have problems getting insurance coverage at all. It is as if infertility is a mark on one's health, which each individual has an obligation to keep clean. Jessica and Doug are a relatively young couple in their late twenties who met while they were attending a college in the Midwest. In Zlín, they became fast friends with April and Larry. Like April and Larry, they were doing IVF with their own eggs, which, ironically, necessitates a longer, three-week stay. Jessica and Doug had recently moved to a small town, where he was a youth minister. While Doug was trying to fend off a terrible cold, Jessica told me how she and her college sweetheart had gone through an embryo adoption program and then realized when they moved to a new town that insurance companies did not want to take them on as clients. As Jessica explained it: "Our infertility is 'on our record.' Certain insurance agencies have told us, 'We can't pick you up within two years of any kind of infertility treatment,' because what they don't want is multiple babies. Because multiples are somewhat common with these types of things, they don't want to be stuck with triplets in the NICU [neonatal intensive care unit] for three months, so they make these rules." Interestingly, as the broker Petra pointed out, when insurance does cover IVF, the price suddenly drops. Typically, insurance companies contract with clinics and pharmacies for prices that are lower than patients' out-of-pocket prices.

The couples I interviewed were quoted various prices for IVF in the United States. They often found clinics that gave low baseline prices but then tacked on fees for medications, donor sperm, donor egg, ICSI, and freezing embryos, as happened for Faith and Michael. Jenny remembered how her quoted baseline price skyrocketed from $10,000 to a final cost of $55,000: "[We] looked into donor eggs, which, you know, $55,000. Well, first they say it's $10,000, and then you go in there and they give you the four-page report. You are flipping the pages and flipping the pages, and there's the bottom line, $55,000. Like, what happened to the $10,000? Oh that's just for this part. . . . So it's like, OK, let's forget that, that's not an option." April remembers the quoted price of $10,000 to $14,000 for a cycle using her eggs, but that did not include ICSI or the blood work.

I met Tom and Hana, owners of IVF Holiday, in the summer of 2008, when I drove to a small town in Ohio to visit with them. Tom is a large, middle-aged man, and we bonded over topics like football during lunch at a chain restaurant. When I interviewed them separately in their home the next day, he explained to me how expensive reproductive care is in the United States. In addition to the sheer cost, Tom characterized the general experience with American infertility treatment as one that entails endless consumption. He presented the following scenario:

> The bottom line is, they knew going in, more than likely, is you're going to need IVF. But they end up nickel-and-diming you with these surgeries. They go to IUIs and all these little things that nickel-and-dime you, and you don't have any money. And oh, $15,000, you've got to do IVF, that's the only way. Say you scrape up the money and you do IVF. Well, now you're thirty-eight, thirty-nine years old, it doesn't work. Well you know what, you're getting kind of up there, your egg quality is not quite what it should be. Thirty thousand dollars, egg donor, and it's almost like they're in sales. Out of pure economics, the sky's the limit on that.

Unfortunately, according to Tom and many others, there is no incentive for fertility clinics in the United States to lower the cost of treatment, given the demand from couples willing and able to pay $50,000 for a cycle. It quickly becomes obvious that the economic reality of reproductive medicine in the United States exiles many patients. The lower middle class is denied treatment options. Despite the fact that women keep trying, working hard to reach their goals of having a family, the system undermines their efforts, making treatment impossible and unaffordable.

Care as Precious Commodity

As couples near the end of treatment options in North America, they grow more disillusioned. They lose faith in North American doctors, who are seen as profiting from their inability to conceive. Of course, couples' alienation is compounded by their lack of success. Although hope and the notion of hard work initially sustain couples, they begin to need more from their health care providers. They need empathy. In other case studies, such as ones involving people who are managing their diabetes, patients often mention feeling that their "personal experiences were not attended to . . . they would have appreciated more interaction and more support" (Mol 2008:97).

Nearly all of my North American informants who had visited a clinic at home commented on the design of the clinic. Built-in aquariums, plush couches, and marble columns signaled excess. Allan, an accountant, and Alida, a schoolteacher, were the last couple I met in the summer of 2011. They had been taking advantage of the kitchen in their room at the pension and so had been making their own meals to save money, which means I did not meet them at breakfast as I did with most couples. When we met again at their home outside of Austin in 2012, Alida joked that her man needed a more substantial breakfast. Alida is Mexican American, while Allan is white and originally from California. They had met through an online dating website. I bumped into the couple in the lobby of the pension when they were getting ready to go to the shopping mall in the town center. They visited the mall every day, since it was air-conditioned and it got them out of the quiet pension. They invited me along, and so we sat on a bench in the mall while they told me their story. They had been turned off by a Houston clinic. Allan remembers, "As soon as you walk in, you walk into white, marble floors with exotic fish tanks. I mean it was up in west Houston, thirty-third floor, with a view over the city. I mean . . . and they want $25,000. You know, we're breaking our backs to try and have these babies, and they're living high on the hog. I was not happy about that." Couples interpret lavish clinic waiting rooms as signs of the profit motives of fertility doctors, and they become even more embittered by the high price tag of ARTs.

Maria and Ryan are from Memphis. I split my time between two Czech towns in the summer of 2010 and had already left Zlín, but when I received an e-mail from Maria, an "expert" reproductive traveler, I decided to travel by train back to the quiet town to meet the couple, who were on their third trip. Maria and Ryan had known one another in high school and reconnected when she ran into him at a Walmart back home. When they talked to me outside the pension, Maria equated North American high costs with cold care:

> It was $16,000 to start, and then it was another $4,000 for the medication, and that was for your basic put everything in a dish and hope everything happens, nothing spectacular. They wanted another $1,600 for ICSI. They wanted $1,000 for medical consultation, where they tell me how to administer my own shots. They wanted $500 for every sperm analysis. I mean they just started rackin' up, and before we knew it, we were looking at right about $30,000. . . . Their bedside manner is absolutely terrible, they don't care if you get pregnant or not. To me, it's more like you're a walking paycheck or a walking ATM is more like it, where they can just keep billing you for everything, and they don't care. They don't care what kind of struggle you're going through or how you have to rearrange your finances. They just, they just don't care at all. It feels very cold, mechanical.

Overwhelmingly, patients felt as if they had been treated like a "number." The idea that one is treated like a number implies that one has been dehumanized, that one's individual situation is not considered; one has not been attended to or, more important, *cared* for. Jana, a Czech clinic coordinator, imagined North American clinics to be like supermarket delis where you have to take a number before going in, since she had heard this expression so often from North American couples. Most couples I spoke to also thought care was lacking. Tracy from California angrily claimed: "I think it's more that they are looking to cash in. It's really expensive. They don't tend to listen to you, even if you're paying all this . . . money out to them. So your appointment's often late, they're barely interested in getting you in, getting you into their system, taking your money off you. And if it works, it works. If it doesn't, it doesn't."

Ironically, once a woman has a failed cycle, the price for further treatment increases. When Alison was contemplating going for another cycle in Minneapolis, the clinic suggested that she and her husband refinance their home: "When they talked about the estimate, we asked if they had a payment plan. Of course that was my husband's first [question]: 'Well, do you have a payment plan?' They suggested refinancing our home. That was what they said to do." Shocked, I nervously laughed, and she continued, "You laugh, but the next clinic, that's the same exact thing that they said. The first thing we asked was 'Do you have a payment plan?' and they said, 'We suggest refinancing your home.' Well, in a market like this."

Besides the perceived blatant cold treatment of doctors, Allan felt as if doctors' arrogance implied that they were above their patients. He said, "He's the only IVF/ob-gyn in the Austin area and he had an attitude like he was helping us, but he was very surly to us. His attitude was 'I'm going to help you, but I'm not going to go out of my way.'" My patient informants did not sense any advocacy on the part of their doctors. Janice and Craig felt as if there was a general lack of concern, given that the clinic never followed through with their care, not even with a phone call after Janice's failed cycle. As Craig described it, "In the IVF treatment we received in the States I felt more like I was walking behind them." My patient informants experienced alienation and felt disconnected from their health care providers.

My survey respondents, clients of IVF brokers who had traveled to the Czech Republic prior to 2010, generally complained about the dearth of care in the United States. They reported being treated as "too old," impersonally, or in a rushed manner by arrogant doctors. Claudia, who has been a nurse for a long time, remembers not feeling "connected" to her specialist. Even though he had worked with her and Ben for a year, she still "felt like there was some withheld information that we didn't get."

Petra remembers distinctly when a nurse left a message on her voicemail that she would need IVF: "The clinic I was seeing here in Atlanta, where I started in 2005, I just got so furious when my coordinator . . . Well, first of all, you call, you get the receptionist, she gets your name, forwards you to the nurse, where you leave a message, and they will call you back once they pull the file." Here, she speaks directly to the bureaucratic nature of the North American health care system in which she is rarely able to actually speak with a human being. She continues:

> Well, this nurse loved to call me on Friday at 4:00 p.m. whenever it is time for her to go home, and I was her last phone call. This one time I was waiting for the results of my HCG test in your tubes to see if they are blocked. So I was waiting for the results, walking around with my cell phone, and I guess I was in a dead zone or something. I guess the phone didn't ring. It just beeped that I got a message. And it was her: "This is such and such leaving you a message for the results of the HCG and it looks like there probably is an occlusion . . . . and you will definitely need an IVF." She just showered me with this information, on a voicemail, Friday at four o'clock. I was immediately trying to call her back, freaking out. What do you mean? What are you saying? And that's when I didn't know what IVF was; I knew IVF was this big black cloud that you don't want to get under. And she leaves me this impersonal, scary voicemail. I was just shaking the whole weekend, and I had to wait till Monday to get some answers. I think I got all of my gray hair right there. It was horrible. It was horrible.

In this and other descriptions, North American clinics are characterized as cold, mechanical, profitable, and uncaring enterprises.

Medical anthropologists have documented the power that the biomedical doctor assumes in our culture, where his or her white coat and specialized knowledge confer an unequal power relationship in the clinical setting (Blumhagen 2009). Kate is a petite woman from Orlando who had worked in a hospital as a speech therapist for several years. She and I bonded over the fact that we both lived in Florida, and she was also a friend of Alison's. She spoke rapidly and clearly. She labeled our health care system "fear based," with doctors dictating the treatment protocols to patients: "In the States we feel like care is dictated to you, and it's a very fearful situation. It feels so out of control. Things aren't done properly; at least, at our clinic they weren't done properly. So it was a lot of fear-based decision making, and stressful." The doctor in the traditional biomedical paradigm has all the information, and patients are seeking this specialized knowledge. Patients are aware of this power imbalance. As couples become more and more jaded with the North American baby business, many begin to question the doctor's authority. As patients come to see the fertility clinic as a business and the doctors as entrepreneurs, they begin to question their doctor's traditional knowledge power.

My North American informants, dissatisfied with cold treatment, arrogant doctors, the traditional paradigm, and their own depleted savings accounts, felt they had reached the end of any hope of conceiving a child via ARTs in the States. They had exhausted their savings, perhaps remortgaged their houses, and found treatment provisions unacceptable given the exorbitant prices. We can interpret care as a missing element from the North American baby business model, a precious yet absent commodity. North American infertile couples struggling mentally, physically, and financially demand a certain kind of compassionate care as a central element to any further treatment. Given the value of hard work and perseverance, lower-middle-class North Americans turn from these closed doors to find other options. They suddenly become patient-consumers having to maneuver in a global health care market, where they have to do even more hard work to find treatment possibilities. The following chapter traces the next stage of their journey.

2

Virtual Communities and Markets

After the IVF Vacation experience, I cannot understand why
anyone would opt to pay $30,000 plus dollars for the U.S.A.
IVF donor option when they will receive the same level of
medical support in the Czech Republic plus have a wonderful vacation for less than half the cost of the U.S. IVF donor
program!
—Anonymous blog

As we have seen, lower-middle-class infertile couples are often angry
and frustrated by the high-priced North American "baby business" and
begin to question the medical care provided by doctors. Jenny, disillusioned by doctors' greed and failure to care, turned to the Internet. She
told me: "We decided there has to be some other option, somebody's not
telling us something. So [we] start Googling. Unfortunately for doctors
in the U.S., we have the Internet now. So patients can take matters into
their own hands. They used to be able to tell us whatever and we'd heed
it. Now we don't need to anymore. Now we can get our own information
and do things for ourselves."

When a person like Jenny goes online seeking information related
to a medical issue, she is embracing a neoliberal model of health care.[1]
This model includes the following elements: no government regulation
or offering of public services, plus a freeing of borders and constraints
to allow for the mobility of capital, people, and services on a global scale.
This model of profit-driven health care has been exported around the
world, whereby health is viewed as a commodity (Whittaker, Manderson, and Cartwright 2010:337). As described by Stone, "Global capitalism has meant an increasing linking of local, small-scale economies into
a broader international economy dominated by multinational corporations. These corporations are oriented toward profits, economic growth,
and the commoditization of more and more goods and services. . . . a

global economy based on what has been called 'neoliberalism'. . . favors unrestricted world trade, privatization, and less interference of governments generally in the economy" (2014:292).

Neoliberal policies of health care have shifted the values people hold concerning their health. Individual responsibility is a central value that has replaced community or public good. As health care services are commoditized, patients become consumers who must be diligent when making choices within a global market of health care. Reproductive travelers see themselves as consumers, and they can choose among various interrelated resources as they make plans to travel abroad for IVF (Becker 2000). Metzl and Kirkland's *Against Health* (2010) reveals the ways in which the medical industrial complex, seeking patients to consume particular products in their endless search for "health," creates a framework in which patients are consumers. Furthermore, the various ways patients act as consumers are often framed in terms of "moral responsibility" for one's health, and the extent to which patients consume is reflected in moral judgments against the individual.

The proliferation of choices—read as new possibilities—is empowering. Most North Americans I met during my research embraced this value of individual responsibility. Jenny, quoted earlier, and other women I met found the Internet to be enabling, as it opened doors to worlds of information that were once restricted. However, while people may experience their choices as liberating, that does not preclude the possibility that they are also entering new arrangements of power whose ramifications are not fully perceived (Abu-Lughod 1990). As Rose asserts, "The obligations of knowledge and choice are onerous enough" (2007:95).

Prainsack, critically examining the powerful rhetoric of patient empowerment as it is celebrated by the mass media, rightly argues that "genuine patient 'empowerment' requires, first, the provision of publicly funded and regulated infrastructures that *de facto* enable choice, and that enable access to appropriate care" (2014: 21). The expectations of North American patients extend only to wanting more choices and never quite reach the level of demand for access to affordable care in the United States. It is time-consuming for patients to research possible clinics or brokers, and there is a high level of uncertainty as they traverse this uncharted terrain. The reproductive traveler is the "global biological citizen, embodying a neoliberal dream," according to Andrea Whittaker (2008:283). Michael Nahman correctly points out that "neoliberal choice is a fallacy" and that a woman's sense of autonomy points to "the story of how globalization and capitalism work on people" (2013:55).

Just as there are obvious contradictory aspects of reproductive technologies for women, the Internet as a tool for patient activism is also highly contradictory. As patients embrace increased levels of personal responsibility for their own health care, they are working hard yet again. As described by Rose, "Every citizen must now become an active partner in the drive for health, accepting their responsibility for securing their own well-being" (2007:63). Furthermore, the decision-making process involved in embarking on a global journey of conception entails a great deal of stress.

As women "do the research" (Speier 2011a), conducting endless Google searches for options, they come across IVF brokers, join support groups, read blogs, and meet others on the road of infertility. The research they conduct can be likened to other types of kinship work that has been shown as gendered (di Leonardo 1987). These websites must be considered not only sites of support but also sites of consumer reports and activism. Yet patients also "increasingly take an active and dynamic role in enhancing their biomedical scientific literacy," all the while claiming empowerment (Whittaker 2008:283). North Americans pushed out by the high costs of IVF join these "biosocial communities" as they begin to imagine other options for fertility treatment (Rose and Novas 2005:450). As explained earlier, "biological citizenship" refers to the roles people assume in relation to their health and sickness. As they conduct Google searches, they engage in "digital biocitizenship" in their quests for parenthood, since their research is conducted online. Their use of the Internet is, again, undergirded by global neoliberal ideologies about individual responsibility for one's own health. Clarke et al. speak of digital capitalism and the Internet as key devices and technologies of biomedicalization (2003:176). As various platforms of social media offer consumers information about health and illness, the Internet is a prime site where we can witness new sites of patient discussion, activism, and information gathering about infertility as a disease.

Reproductive travel is marketed via the Internet, producing new types of patients who self-coordinate their reproductive travels using information gleaned from IVF brokers, blogs, and support groups. Scholars have written about online communities and examined the relationships that develop among people of those communities (Snodgrass, Dengah, and Lacy 2014:481). The virtual, biosocial communities forming on the Web must be considered what Kleinman classically described more than thirty-five years ago as "lay referral groups" (1980), now transposed to digital forms of communication (see also Polat 2012:221). However, these groups have shifted. Gibbon and Novas write, "Novel forms of what might be described as 'lay expertise,' 'activism' and/or 'citizenship' are discernible . . . where there are identifiable transformations in the types of institutional relations that prevail between patients, medical professionals and scientists" (2008:8). There is a new "heterogeneity of knowledge sources" that Clarke et al. interpret as "disrupting the division of 'expert' and 'lay' knowledges and enabling new social linkages" (2003:177). These virtual networks of patients enable women to learn about reproductive travel and potential destination sites for IVF. The women educate one another about their shared infertility experiences and learn the technological jargon that accompanies the world of reproductive medicine. These biosocial communities are central for women, who, as noted earlier, are the primary actors in these gendered worlds. As in a case in Turkey, similar fertility support websites were a "specific form of women's gathering" (Polat 2012:215). Women build and sustain friendships when they share confidential information with one another and have similar experiences. As they speak with other women who have pursued treatment abroad, they essentially become lay experts. Polat understands the Internet as a site of the "production of scientific knowledge on the basis of [patients'] own experiences" (201). Ultimately, patients who participated in my study discovered the IVF brokers' web-based companies.

It is important to consider the virtual communities of women seeking support, information, and encouragement to travel abroad. "Interactions with and through the Internet are inherently complex and diffuse, defying focus on an easily defined research population that is bound by a particular geographical space" (Lee 2013:552). A handful of scholars have written about the role that brokers play in the global reproductive tourism industry. Gürtin refers to them as "interface agents" (2012:81). Deomampo has written about former surrogates in India who become "agents" for surrogacy, who advocate for patients but also act as entrepreneurs (2013). In a similar yet distinct vein, the IVF brokers for the Czech Republic are former sufferers of infertility.

These IVF brokers are the supply side of a global market of health care. They brand and sell "fertility holidays"—a truly layered package. A nuanced discourse pervades the rhetoric employed by brokers, who assume much of the "stress" related to fertility treatment and travel. The marketing techniques of these brokers are framed as "intimate labor" (Boris and Parreñas 2010), which may be defined as work that entails bodily and emotional closeness as well as intimate knowledge of personal information. IVF brokers are intimately aware of the bodily and emotional toil involved in undergoing in vitro fertilization. Broker websites prey upon patients who are dissatisfied with private medicine in North America, and they promise the hope of a white baby, excellent care, and a vacation. Because the North American baby business is broken in the sense that patients no longer feel cared for, brokers recognize this and step in to relieve the stress of being a consumer in the global marketplace of fertility treatment. Intimate labor is a useful lens through which to grasp the interconnections of economic transactions and the importance of the intimate discourse of "care" that is utilized by medical brokers.

It is important to consider the role that the media play in offering up particular images and fantasies for the tourist's imagination. Crouch, Jackson, and Thompson discuss the ways that the "tourist imagination" is a "kind of bridging concept" to speak to the importance of media as it engenders global gendered mobility of travel (2005:1). Löfgren (1999), borrowing from Appadurai (1996), uses the term "vacationscapes" to speak to the ways that particular vacation spots or landscapes merge with the daydreams of tourists. The IVF broker websites, replete with testimonials, create particular fantasies for reproductive patient tourists. Thus, the imagination that is inculcated by broker websites for reproductive travelers must be taken as a central motivator for their reproductive mobility and becomes an active part of their physical travels given that "both tourism and media text are enmeshed within numerous flows of cultural events, contexts, desires and feeling" (Crouch, Jackson, and Thompson 2005:12). The imaginations that tourists take with them are an active part of their physical travels.

Just as reproductive technologies are technologies of hope, so may the Internet be considered a place to instill more hope for women yearning for a family that fits within heteronormative codes. The Internet is a space where women's "hope is 'kept awake,' 'kept alive'" (Polat 2012:218). It is with fertility tourism that the hope and fantasy of vacation merge with the hope embodied in reproductive technologies. There are symbolic and ideological underpinnings to fertility treatments and tourism; both entail imagination filled with promises.

Fertility Threads

"Stirrup Queens," "Inspire," "RESOLVE," "Fertility Friends"—these are just a few of the online support groups a woman can join along her infertility journey. Proffered reasons for the gendered nature of these virtual communities reflect cultural assumptions about masculinity and femininity. Infertility is considered a woman's problem. While men, too, may be infertile (Inhorn 2012), the hoped-for pregnancy will happen in a woman's body, and femininity is profoundly associated with fertility in the United States and elsewhere. Women are more "open" about personal matters, and thus more likely to seek group as well as individual support. According to norms of femininity, research has shown a gendered pattern of social media usage: 76 percent of women and 66 percent of men are said to use Facebook as social media (Duggan and Smith 2013). Yet the difference widens tremendously when it comes to fertility support groups. Few to no men populate fertility threads. In speaking to North American patients, I asked whether these virtual worlds were gendered, and they all agreed wholeheartedly. For example, referring to one website devoted to North Americans thinking about traveling to the Czech Republic, Faith told me that men constitute fewer than 10 of the 612 members.

A few days before sitting on Faith's couch in rural Georgia, I had driven to South Carolina to meet her close friend Julie. The two women had been in Zlín at the same time. Before my late arrival, Julie's husband had set up a video montage of pictures from their trip to the Czech Republic that played continuously in the background as we talked. They had struggled with infertility for four years. Julie explained to me the gendered nature of online support groups: "I think mostly because it's actually mostly happening to the wives. I think men . . . it's kind of like planning a wedding. Men are just happy to show up, you know. From my perspective, that's what I've found out so far." The next day Faith agreed, claiming infertility affects women on a daily basis:

> For the women it's more. For instance, when my husband and I first started trying to have children, and got serious about it, I would take the medication every day. I would take my temperature every day. It was affecting me daily. It affects the women more. You go to any gathering, and what do women talk about? Their children. You go to a gathering of men, they talk about their jobs. So it's more, our children are our lives for us women. You get up throughout the night. You deal with your monthly cycle. It affects every part of your social life.

Other anthropologists (van Balen and Inhorn 2002) have revealed how infertility affects women and men in different ways. In Egypt, for example, Inhorn (1994) has shown that women are the ones who are subjected to the physical, psychological, and social pressure to bear a child. The labeling of infertility as a woman's problem drives the gendered nature of virtual biosocial communities, since it is through the Internet that women learn about global routes to parenthood.

A few of my informants, both men and women, laughed at the idea of men going online to share their depression over their low sperm count. Ben, using a sports analogy, said that women are more driven to seek support, while men sit "on the sidelines." Women are "wired" to talk about their issues, he told me, while among men there is an epidemic of silence. Much of this discourse naturalizes women's behavior as emotionally laden, and women have participated in support groups in the past, but the virtual nature of these communities is relatively new. The Internet also perpetuates the gendered nature of infertility.

Similar to cybercommunities that develop around the issue of Chinese adoption, as Anagnost has described, the Internet has the power to "produce new forms of sociality and community" (2004:145). Just as in the case of those who are suffering infertility, "parents enter from a position of soliciting information, but as they proceed through the adoption process, they can then begin to turn more toward sharing information with others" (146). The Internet as a place to network and make connections enables "the pluralization of knowledge production and an expansion and diversification of actors involved in the health sector, paralleled by an increasing activation of patients/consumers" (Polat 2012:200).

Furthermore, just as ARTs can be both empowering and disempowering for infertile women, joining these biosocial worlds of support can also be Janus-faced. Many brokers, doctors, and husbands expressed concern about the amount of time women spent online. As we talked, Daniel, from Los Angeles, struggled slightly as he tried to articulate the complicated nature of these sites. He described the two sides of online forums: "There's a lot of hope on there and advice on the forum, because it's all a bunch of women wanting themselves and other women to succeed. There is that sort of negative pall that sort of hangs over the whole thing of people that tried it and it didn't work out. That's not something that I want to talk about."

Women who initially land upon websites of support may "lurk" before joining. A woman's level of participation will ebb and flow as she moves along her journey. In her years of being a broker, Petra had become critical of the forums for being full of "too much estrogen," and Jenny, though she championed the use of Google, characterized the women online as "lamenters." Here, we note that women who participate in virtual communities walk a fine line and may face approbation if they participate too heavily. It is as if women are expected to continue to work hard, go online to seek information and resources, yet never wallow or succumb to the depressing side of infertility. There is a femininity/fertility police that is enforcing gender norms that urge women to maintain a semblance of hope for a family.

Given the tidal nature of women's participation, fertility threads will split, and some blogs fall into favor while others fizzle out. When I asked Petra of IVF Choices which sites she would recommend, she said, "It changes so often. Something that I found a few months ago is not there, and something else is not there. So I wouldn't recommend a specific site to go to, but always try to do a fresh search." Ultimately, it is through such blogs and support groups that women learn about reproductive travel. One husband joked that his wife had found out about reproductive travel on eBay, which highlights the global, consumer framework of fertility medicine. Once a woman hears about this phenomenon, she will try to learn more.

Diligent Patient-Consumers

Who knew that a Google search late one night would lead us
halfway across the world in our quest for a baby?
—Anonymous blog

In addition to the support women seek online, these sites are important
sources of information. Furthermore, "New information technologies
and the massive increase in the participation of the media in forming
public awareness, especially with regard to health issues and technological developments, [have] brought about a 'new informed patient' who
is handling the available knowledge him or herself" (Polat 2012:207).
"Doing the research" involved the endless information women gather
from support groups, brokers, and clinic websites. Valerie and Dan,
whom I met at the clinic, decided they did want children after she miscarried their unplanned pregnancy. As we sat outside soaking up the
sun, and later over dinner at an Irish-themed pub, Valerie continually
spoke about "doing the research" when looking into options for fertility treatment. "Doing the research" entails conducting endless online
searches. Valerie said she conducted "Google searches—yeah, tons and
tons and tons of Google searches. You can probably look at my cookies
and there's thousands of crazy searches." Interestingly, another Cali-
fornian, Dan, labeled his wife's endless searching as "Google-fu," again
utilizing a sports metaphor in speaking of his wife's expertise.

These Google searches can be linked to what Mol has called the
"logic of choice," as opposed to the "logic of care" (2008:1). Mol argues
that the logic of care is under threat as choice increasingly becomes
the ideal for patients. However, she points out that making choices is
time-consuming, and it can also be understood as a disciplining tech-
nique. Indeed, "in the logic of choice, having a choice implies that one
is responsible for what follows" (Mol 2008:91). This reinforces a North
American patient's responsibility for her own health.

Because it is perceived as a moral imperative for women wanting to get
pregnant to be vigilant about their health, Faith spoke as if it were also a
moral imperative that women do their own research about reproductive
options. As women actively seek information about IVF options, they
embrace this moral duty, which is a continuation of the moral impera-

tive that women work hard in trying to solve the problem of infertility. Doing such research is a "healthy" usage of social media. Valerie spoke of having to figure out one's IVF options as "work," painting the scenario as if doctors withhold information from patients: "You tend to have to do a lot of work on your own, to find out facts, 'cause they don't give you all the options." These patients are being diligent consumers as they collect information from various sources about other possible treatments.

I interviewed Zoe via Skype in the fall of 2010. She lives in Barbados, a small island in the Caribbean that was preparing for a possible hurricane at the time. A British citizen, Zoe was well versed in medical travel, having previously traveled to New Jersey for general care, given the limited medical facilities on the island. Zoe talked about her research in great detail. She said it was a three-stage process online. The first stage was gathering general information about reproductive technologies. During that stage, Zoe said, "It was a Google search: 'What do you ask a reproductive endocrinologist at your first meeting?' And it took me to the website of 'Stirrup Queens.' There was just amazing information there on the types of questions that you should ask. Then, of course, it had the links to the blogs, and ultimately to their monthly column where you visit other people's blogs. So that was sort of like my first introduction to a whole world of information on the Internet." Zoe then described her next stage: "To peoples' blogs who were looking to go overseas for IVF. I was able to read about different experiences in different countries. So that was sort of like the second stage of it. The third stage I had actually joined 'IVF Connections,' because I just really wanted to get specific information related to certain countries. . . . I can go and do a search on any other place that started to come up. And at that point, the Czech Republic board was really good." In the end, Zoe joined "IVF Connections," since it was geared toward North American women. The Czech pages contained endless patient testimonials, which essentially can be considered consumer reports, praising the treatment they received in the Czech Republic, at a fraction of the price they would have to pay at home. As patients like Zoe navigate through various websites, they inevitably come across IVF broker websites.

Branding Fertility Holidays

Julie remembers when she first saw the website for IVF Holiday: "I said a little prayer that it wouldn't crash my computer, and I clicked." She said that she often tells this joke, which reveals the level of uncertainty patients inevitably feel as they first hear of and explore fertility tourism. It also indicates the extent to which this global medical industry is completely unregulated, allowing space for new kinds of businesses like medical brokers to capture and profit from consumer demand. Ultimately, once patients land upon IVF broker websites, virtual marketplaces for fertility holidays, they enter a new realm of hope in their quests for parenthood. In this marketplace of medicine, "marketing is a matter of seduction . . . a remarkable way of playing with desires" (Mol 2008:29–30).

The two main brokers for North Americans at the time of this research were IVF Holiday, owned by Tom and Hana of Ohio, and IVF Choices, owned by Petra in Atlanta. I learned about reproductive travel to the Czech Republic from a colleague who saw a story about IVF Holiday. I arranged to meet with Tom and Hana at a Bob Evans restaurant in the summer of 2008. Tom and Hana, who had been interviewed by CNN and other news stations, probably initially lumped me with journalists. As a young Czech woman, Hana had met Tom online on a music sharing website. After communicating online for several weeks, they began talking on the phone. Hana was from a small town in Moravia, eastern Czech Republic; Tom was from a small town in Ohio, where he worked for the family business. Eventually, Hana flew to the United States to meet Tom; they hit it off and were married within a year.

Like many North American couples that marry for a second or third time, Tom had a teenage son from a previous marriage and had had a vasectomy. Younger than Tom, Hana wanted her own children, so Tom underwent a vasectomy reversal, which alone can be costly. However, their doctor said they would still need to do IVF. When they were quoted a price of more than $10,000 for treatment in the United States, they were devastated. Like the couples we met in chapter 1, they knew Tom's middle-class salary alone would not be enough to pay for treatment. Hana decided to visit a Czech clinic during one of her annual visits home.

Luckily, Hana's first cycle of IVF led to the birth of twin girls. Buoyed by their success, Tom and Hana talked about helping other lower-middle-class North Americans travel to the Czech Republic, where they could take advantage of the lower prices of Czech reproductive medicine. Four months pregnant, Hana began to make arrangements with several places of accommodation and the clinic where she had been treated. When Dr. R., head of the clinic, narrated the beginning of his relationship with IVF Holiday, he said Hana was very "wise" in creating her website, which she called "IVF Holiday." Suddenly, patients diligently conducting research online would land upon this broker website, where they are greeted by a picture of Tom and pregnant Hana, the happy ending to their infertility story implicit from the first glance at her expanding belly. Images of postage stamps and European travel destinations adorn the background of the website, alongside pictures of beautiful castles, lush scenery, and the most effective testimonial of Czech IVF: a picture of Tom and Hana's twins smiling at the bottom of their personal story.

In the first few months of their business, Hana was approached by a woman, Petra, who was another Czech married to a North American. Petra proffered a partnership, which Tom and Hana declined. In May 2006, they were appalled to discover a website, "IVF Choices," that mimicked their business model. Petra also worked with a clinic in Moravia. Like Hana, Petra networked with various hotels in Brno and contracted with an apartment her mother managed. Unlike Hana, however, she earned an exclusive contract with the clinic, which benefited tremendously from gaining foreign clientele. The sudden appearance of these two broker companies whose business models mirrored each other reflects the extent to which this medical tourism industry is highly competitive.

Both brokers rely upon their families abroad as an important component in this global care chain. Hana's father drives clients to and from the airport, and Petra's mother manages an apartment building that is often used as accommodations by IVF Choices' clients. As I have argued, "Their transnational kinship ties form the foundation for North American reproductive travel to the Czech Republic" (Speier 2015:31).

Both IVF brokers promise couples a "low-stress" IVF cycle in a beautiful setting where couples can enjoy a European vacation. Their websites are adorned with cherubic, smiling, blue-eyed babies, and they promise a plenitude of egg donors with Caucasian features and a technologically up-to-date clinic with doctors who *care*. Petra's website reads: "The IVF medical staff is personal, kind and focused on individual attention, with the goal of reducing the emotional stress of couples trying to get pregnant through in vitro fertilization." Embedded in this marketing scheme is a product that differs radically from that of North American fertility medicine. Brokers are well aware of lower-middle-class dissatisfaction with high costs and promise their clients a better experience overall. Aware of the stress associated with IVF, they even promise better success rates.

In January 2006, IVF Holiday trademarked its website and began arranging travel to Zlín, Czech Republic. The beginning was slow going until the company's first clients gave birth; their successful cycle and testimonial propelled the business. By 2008, IVF Holiday was sending five to fourteen couples to the clinic each month, with business steadily growing for several years. The company advertised on Yahoo and Google and received national attention from news companies, anthropologists, blogs, and many patients. In these first few years, any North American couple that wanted to go to the Czech Republic for IVF had to use the services of IVF Holiday. Broker rates varied from $399 to $3,000, and couples could choose from different packages and services. Once the business had had enough successful cycles, clients provided testimonials, which became the mainstay in terms of advertising fertility tourism.

Testimonials on these websites promise couples they can travel to the Czech Republic, where they will find affordable yet excellent care. They can enjoy a European vacation, with the promise of the best souvenir: a baby. Baby pictures are the "proof" of effective ARTs in the Czech Republic. Testimonials enable women or couples to imagine themselves traveling abroad, as they identify with other "average" women who face the same struggles of infertility. Claudia identified with a woman of her same profession whose testimonial she read online: "I went and read all about the people, what they had to say about it. There was a doctor in there. There was a nurse like me. They were from California. So I was noting the type of people that were able or willing to go, even though they didn't know what the place was like. So that helped." In fact, the most legitimizing testimonials are from people in the health care profession.

The key element encased within reviews of Czech clinics is the "care" that North Americans are ultimately seeking. Cindy said that after she read so many blogs and testimonials about the Czech clinic, she was trusting: "After reading what all the ladies said about this clinic. They take such good care of you. I really wasn't worried." What is striking is the number of couples who claim, like Cindy, that after talking to previous clients they were worry free, despite the fact that they were about to travel such a long distance and encounter a different language, national culture, and health care system. Maria remembers her first trip to Zlín: "It was worry free. We knew when we got here we would have someone to translate. On their website they have pictures of the clinic and the staff so you knew what to expect. We knew Lucko was going to be there to translate, we knew the doctors and some of the staff spoke English, it was almost worry free." The fact that she qualifies her statement with the word "almost" indicates that there may have been some stress involved in traveling to the Czech Republic for IVF.

In addition to the promise of excellent care, couples must also be assured that Czech technological standards are equal to those in North America. Photos of Czech clinics pepper broker websites, offering up performances of technology in images of sonogram machines and embryologists smiling in front of large microscopes. Couples are assured that the medical standards are excellent, through pictures of smiling doctors in scrubs. Lauren had worried that the significantly lower cost would mean they would receive less advanced treatment:

> At first, just wondering if the cost that we're saving was gonna compromise the procedure and the care. That was my main concern. Yes, I wanted to save money, but not at the cost of it not working. In talking to Tom and Hana and Faith and different people, and just hearing about the clinic put my mind at ease. They are up to date with all the technology and everything with in vitro. Seeing pictures of the clinic. It looked very up to date and didn't look outdated at all. That was kind of my main concern.

Again: care, a worry-free cycle, and technical competence are concerns of these global consumers who must make complicated decisions with respect to their fertility treatment. They assume the responsibility of checking these factors, sifting through the layers of a fertility package.

One woman blogged, "Being a diligent consumer, I did some research and spoke to former clients. They were all thrilled with the service that they received and talked about being treated with dignity and respect. Even more, they all talked about what a wonderful time they had on their IVF 'vacation.' They seemed to all be impressed with the clinic and doctors—whose success rates are equivalent to most clinics here in the U.S.—but at a fraction of the cost." Women and couples usually process the idea of traveling abroad for IVF for at least a few weeks, if not longer. During this time, they must be smart consumers who research the product they are thinking about buying: a fertility holiday. The plethora of testimonials frames expectations for future North American reproductive travelers, who decide to embark on a journey halfway around the globe in their quest for parenthood. Building on their experiences in North American fertility clinics, couples who have been highly dissatisfied with what they perceived as a lack of care are drawn to the promise of caring doctors and nurses at the Czech clinic.

Strangely, and at odds with this active research mode, some women I met spoke of "stumbling upon" or randomly "coming across" websites in their initial foray into virtual communities of infertility. Given the stigmatized nature of infertility, most women felt as if they had no one to ask for information. They eventually "stumble upon" information after relentless searching. They also spoke of happenstance meetings with strangers. At a clinic in Minneapolis, Alison met a woman who told her about the possibility of IVF abroad. She recalled: "So, we were on the elevator in the reproductive wing, and there was a lady, she looked like she was about seven, eight months pregnant. I made a comment about IVF or something. She said, 'Well, I shouldn't relay this to you, but . . .' She said that she had a failed attempt so then she went through IVF Holiday. She said a friend of hers had seen it on CNN and called her." Information about reproductive travel is a secret hidden from patients by doctors, yet passed along surreptitiously in the halls of North American clinics or in the virtual communities of support. It is as if "stumbling upon" websites aligned reproductive travel with fate.

Lauren and John were relatively young and from Texas. I appreciated John's sarcasm; Lauren remained more soft-spoken. She had told me about turning to her church for support when she first dealt with infertility. Lauren spoke of finding out about reproductive travel as an opportunity that they had not actively sought out: "When this opportunity came up, we thought, well, 'We didn't seek it out, it came to us.' So we just took it as an opportunity and a chance." Once introduced to the idea, patients once again assume a proactive research mode. They contact former clients. The culmination of hard work and luck and timing are painted as leading a couple closer to the reproductive travel route to the Czech Republic. In fact, it is again a "neo-liberal consumer discourse that promotes being 'proactive' and 'taking charge' of one's health" (Clarke et al. 2003:181).

Propelled by dissatisfaction with North American clinics' profit motives and lack of care, North Americans are seeking low-cost care, effective technologies, and white donors from their fertility travel package. I believe that the "care" that is being marketed via medical tourism is ultimately central in the global marketplace (Cabezas 2011). There is a global menu of IVF options: Spain, Mexico, South Africa, India, Thailand. Yet the marketing by IVF brokers encapsulates key criteria. One blog listed a couple's reasons for choosing the Czech Republic through IVF Holiday: "We researched many different countries and clinics and ultimately chose this one for the following: (1) the donor would have similar physical features (2) the medical practices in general in Czech Republic were much more advanced than some of the other countries we considered (3) cost (4) first-hand feedback from others that had used this clinic." So, essentially, couples are seeking white babies, advanced technologies, lower costs, and a holiday. Cost is not the main reason people choose to travel to the Czech Republic, but rather it figures into a confluence of factors, varying levels of motivation, and desire. Similar to North American patient-consumers, Nahman writes of Israeli Jews who also privilege "Europeanness" in seeking racialized egg donation, labeling IVF a "technology of racism" whereby the particular traits that recipients want tend to "involve European notions of beauty" (2013:118).

Assuming the Work of Travel

During my first week in Zlín, Hana was kind enough to coordinate a meeting with some of her clients who were also in town. I met Juan and

Anita, from Indianapolis, at a pizzeria for lunch, and then we enjoyed iced coffees next door. Juan and Anita had been impressed with IVF Holiday; the brokers were prompt and knowledgeable and did a lot of research for them. Brokers help arrange travel itineraries, offer transportation to and from the airport as well as within the country, and provide translation services. Because traveling abroad involves a lot of planning, brokers handle these arrangements, showing couples how to find cheap airfare, arranging clinic visits and hotel stays, and assuming much of the burden of planning. Juan and Anita liked it that Hana did most of the research for them. Juan said, "They had it set up like third parties. Hana helped us with a lot of work. We don't have to. We just call her instead of having to do it." They are travel agents for a particular type of fertility holiday that bundles hope, low-price treatment, relaxation, and excellent health care.

In making travel arrangements, brokers are trying to lessen the stress couples experience. Brokers are the lubrication in the global gears of reproductive medicine. Making the process "smooth" was an oft-repeated description of the coordinator's job, as Jana, one of Petra's Czech coordinators, described it: "To basically make everything smoother, or just help them out with anything they might need. To make it easier for them. Especially to collect them to the clinic, to help them, and just take care of them and help them with anything they might need."

In hiring IVF brokers, couples do not entirely relinquish their responsibility for their treatment. The brokers are framed as "informal liaisons." Though they may be informal, I argue they are essential in paving this global care route. In the beginning, most North American patients would not have considered traveling to the Czech Republic without the assistance of an IVF broker. April and Larry found the existence of IVF Holiday to be a legitimating factor of the Czech reproductive travel industry. As Larry explained: "There was some sort of comfort in knowing there was a company; that was a comfort in the beginning. I know when I tell people I think we might go overseas, one of the first things I would say, 'There's even companies here that help you set it up.'"

The IVF coordinators arrange travel and manage schedules and transportation—essentially, the movement of North Americans through Czech towns and clinics. Floridian Janice claimed that she and her husband, Craig, "like the idea that they follow you from the beginning to the end." This sense of being "followed" becomes relevant after hearing about their experience of not being followed in the States. Janice remembered her cycle in Florida: "There was never a call back, even from the first time we went to one of the offices, the one that did most of the work for us. There was never a call back to see how we were doing. After the insemination, never ever did they call." Janice and Craig appreciated that Hana promised to call them after their first appointment in Zlín, and they expected there would be follow-up even after they returned home.

Brokers not only ensure that travel arrangements go smoothly but also must facilitate a client's IVF cycle. There is detailed bodily coordination that has to occur before a couple leaves for the Czech Republic. The woman's protocol must be written out. Women must take medications and synchronize their cycle with their egg donor and must self-administer shots. The medications are complicated, and they continue while the couple is in the Czech Republic and for months after they return home. Petra explains the process a patient goes through once she decides to travel to Brno for IVF, working with Petra's company IVF Choices:

> I try to walk you through the process, explain everything—what the treatment looks like. We would let you know what tests you need to have done. Mostly, we just ask for the medical history. . . . Then I would send you a contract. I would send you a travel guide with all the information about Czech. We would communicate with the clinic that there is this patient [who] wants to be in Czech from July 1 to July 14. Once you get your blood tests, you start your birth control pills, and you would start working on the travel arrangements. We are working on the travel arrangements, the clinic reviews the medical history and puts together a protocol with the dates: this is what you do on June 15, 16, and 17. Once we begin this protocol, we would go through what the protocol means, what it looks like. Once you get the medications, there will be another phone call, but in the meantime, any questions are answered by phone or via e-mail. Once you get the medications and you actually have them in your hand, we explain to you how it all works. We tell people to set up Skype, so that we can see each other, because it helps.

Petra's role as coordinator here extends far beyond travel arrangements to embrace the patient's body and detailed treatment protocol, which involves intimate details of a woman's cycle. Skype itself becomes an "intimate technology" in augmenting and personalizing the experience of care and medical confidence.

Given the levels of stress women experience in going through treatment in North America, couples find this idea of a vacation and a less stressful clinical encounter appealing. The fact of a global encounter with a new medical system is minimized with the promise of a holiday. This vacation element is also central for ensuring a more cost-effective and successful IVF. Because success rates for IVF hover below 30 percent,[2] people begin to see IVF in North America as a waste, since it occurs in the midst of one's busy, everyday life. A fertility holiday is more cost-effective than a North American cycle. Nearly every couple I met recited similar cost comparisons: Angela and Chris from Chicago said they could do four trips for the price of one cycle at home.

Jessica and Doug, the young couple from the Midwest, admitted that money was their first incentive, but then they started getting excited about the idea of a vacation: "I think our main motivation was the money and that we heard that the clinic was excellent. Then we started getting excited about where can we go? What should we see? Prague, Vienna, all these places that a lot of people go." In reading broker websites, patients read testimonials that assure them they will have a vacation.

The brokers sell reproductive travel by the guarantee not of a successful cycle of IVF but of a vacation. One blog reads:

> It sounds crazy, but John and I agree that it wouldn't have been devastating if we failed our first trip, because we would get to go back and see everyone and everything again. Oh yeah, and shop more! When we had failed cycles in the States (we had many, many failures here) we felt like our money just went to waste. It just evaporated. Even if we didn't get pregnant on our first try in the Czech Republic, our money gave us a great vacation and memories. The Czech Republic is a very easy and beautiful country to travel in, the locals are friendly, a lot of people speak English, and the food is great. Petra will guide you through all the travel and even schedules massages!!

Not many couples had ever thought of traveling to the Czech Republic for a vacation, which IVF brokers realized. They used images of capital cities like Vienna and Budapest to entice them. Brokers package a generic European vacation that includes castles and romantic historic cities. No matter the location, IVF brokers will make the claim that North Americans who truly embrace the vacation aspect will have higher success rates. Of course, there are no statistics to support these claims, but it undergirds their main marketing strategy.

Attentive IVF Brokers

As mentioned earlier, IVF broker companies are owned by Czech-American couples who have suffered infertility. They utilize their experience as a way to express their "attentiveness" to and empathy for couples who are unable to afford treatment in the United States. Hana, founder of IVF Holiday, and Petra, founder of IVF Choices, both suffered infertility, came up against overpriced American fertility medicine, and decided to be "return reproductive tourists" to the Czech Republic (Inhorn 2011). However, these brokers also run companies that are seeking profit. In intimate labor, "workers align their emotions, bodies, and behavior to the goal of profit making" (Ducey 2010:24). Hana and Petra know the emotional suffering of infertility, and they can empathize with their clients. These brokers "assert the primacy of affective relationships in their trade . . . to reassert a discourse of nurture within the commercial relationship" (Whittaker and Speier 2010:373). Using the lens of intimate labor underlines the ways brokers are assuming the care of and responsibility for reproductive travelers.

The IVF brokers must have congenial and empathetic personalities because they are the main contact that a North American will have before traveling abroad. Jana, one of Petra's Czech-based coordinators, spoke of how happy the clients were with Petra: "They love Petra, they love Petra. It is a huge thing, they are very happy that she calls within same day." In fact, Petra was well aware of the importance of "care," and the basis of her compassion is her own experience with infertility. In explaining her dedication to her work, she said: "I guess it just makes a difference because I really do have my heart in it. I have done it all. I mean all ways, all treatments, all the way to surrogacy. I have a lot of personal experience; there is always a difference. Whenever I was going to the clinics here, they're all experts and doctors, but I have not met one that has gone through it themselves yet." Having experienced IVF cycles several times, in North America and the Czech Republic, Petra knew she could empathize with her clients.

When I first met Hana, she said to me, "It's so great how you get attached to people, and when you talk to them . . . you just become more like a friend than a formal client, you know, business relationship." In their narratives, IVF brokers claim satisfaction in the intimacy of their labor, often understating the profit they are earning. The brokers continually speak of how they "care" about their clients, in effect diminishing the attention placed on the market transaction that is occurring. The brokers embody the intersection of intimate labor and a heightened commodification of intimacy. Of course, they are not the only type of worker who is selling care, but this is especially important when so much stress and hope are involved.

The broker websites are replete with testimonials from patients who affirm the affective discourse, speaking glowingly of the care that was provided. Past clients claim they were treated like family. One testimonial reads, "By the time we left, we felt like family. We were continually pampered with personalized service, and special touches, like the 'his and hers' full-body massages, were a treat. We were always kept informed of our progress, and we felt genuinely cared for. . . . Our heartfelt thanks to our new 'Czech family.'" The phrase "Czech family" indicates the affective bonds between brokers and clients. Reproductive travelers conceptualize coordinators in transnational, familial terms. In fact, patients often based their choice of a broker on the sense of "connection" they felt in speaking to one of them. "Connections" are a useful trope for understanding the affective bonds between patients and brokers (see also Speier 2015).

Testimonials from previous clients attest to the care provided by brokers. The relationships created between brokers and clients are based on shared personal intimacies, where clients must talk about bodily processes and substances with brokers, who in turn share intimate bodily secrets of infertility with their clients (Boris and Parreñas 2010:7). The IVF brokers assume much of the stress that patients experience when undergoing treatment. The neoliberal model of health care is stressful for consumers, who at first feel in the dark about infertility. The brokers help to calm patients, ease their minds, and effectively coordinate the entire package.

It is through gendered practices of social media that North Americans discover the possibility of a fertility holiday, where they are promised a relaxing treatment in Europe at a fraction of the price, and a clinical experience where the doctors and nurses truly care about them. All the research women do online in terms of reading IVF broker websites and participating in blog communities is part of the workload of a diligent patient-consumer navigating a global health care market. As women gather information, support one another, and provide testimonials of their trips and experiences, they are forming biosocial communities of infertile patients, continuing the hard work they assumed the moment they were diagnosed as infertile. Maintaining their gendered work associated with infertility, they embark on reproductive journeys. An idealized notion of an American work ethic continues to pervade infertility journey narratives. These hardworking women who opt to travel abroad also claim to be courageous.

It is in these virtual biosocial communities that female patients are becoming lay experts with respect to their infertility and stumbling upon IVF broker websites that offer packaged fertility holidays. The layers imbued in these package deals manipulate the hope that is already embedded in reproductive technologies and enlarge the elemental hope of having a vacation, being able to relax during treatment. They also promise North Americans technological success and caring physicians.

The next chapter follows couples who "take that leap" and end up at a Czech clinic in a small town halfway around the world. They are "pioneers," which is the frontier idiom that Franklin (2013) uses in speaking about the field of reproductive technology. Yet the decision to travel to the Czech Republic is a market-based one, and patients approach it as diligent consumers. The next chapter witnesses their entrance into a clinic far away.

3

Intimate Labor within Czech Clinics

Kay had traveled to the Czech Republic for IVF in 2006. She was a lawyer from the Northeast, and she laughed as she described her first visit to the clinic. She rode in a large, rickety communist-era elevator to the second floor of a very old building. Fearful of the elevator, she hesitated, but Hana encouraged her to take this literal and metaphoric step. Thankfully, the door opened onto the same clinic she had seen on the IVF Holiday website, so Kay felt she had been delivered into safe medical hands.

In 2011, Chris humorously depicted the clinic: "To me it almost seems scripted. It's almost like they have all these extremely attractive miniskirt-wearing . . . It's almost like a Willy Wonka goes to the chocolate factory, except we're going to the IVF factory. It's pristine, you go there (he makes a sound with his mouth as if he were producing bubbles), blows the whistle and here comes [an] Oompa-Loompa around the corner."

When I interviewed Hana and Tom, they recalled visiting her family in Moravia, giddily anxious about the clinic visit for their IVF cycle the next day. As they watched television, a special came on that happened to feature Ladislav Pilka, a Czech celebrity of reproductive medicine who had been part of the team involved in the birth of the first "test-tube" baby, Louise Brown, in England in 1978. Pilka then aided in the first Czech test-tube birth in 1982, which was also the first within the Eastern bloc during the Cold War. In fact, he was the head of the very clinic Tom and Hana were going to the next day. Their hope was buoyed by the television special, since Pilka embodied the technological success and advancement of Czech reproductive medicine.

Assisted reproductive technologies have been a growing field (of medicine and business) in the Czech Republic since the 1990s. By the end of the twentieth century, 4,000 of all births in the Czech Republic were IVF births. In 2007, 5,000 cycles of IVF occurred in the Czech Republic, and this number is increasing. It is estimated that 15 percent of Czech couples suffer infertility (Slepičková and Fučík 2009), and 3.5 percent of Czech babies are born via assisted reproduction.[1]

The globalization of reproductive biotechnologies has created even newer tastes and desires, giving rise to a desire for the bodies of "others" (though their difference is suppressed) (L. Cohen 2002). These inequalities are most dramatically illustrated in a consideration of the marketing of bioavailability, the trade in poor women's bodies for egg donation (Heng 2006, 2007). The phenomenon of cross-border reproductive care reflects a globally "stratified reproduction" that entails "the power relations by which some categories of people are empowered to nurture and reproduce, while others are disempowered" (Colen 1986, cited in Ginsburg and Rapp 1995b:3). There is a class structure within the reproductive industry, by which individuals are ranked and considered appropriate for different reproductive tasks (Tober 2002; Heng 2006, 2007). Compounding this is the fact that often "one woman's possession of reproductive choice may actually depend on or deepen another woman's reproductive vulnerability" (Solinger 2002:7). The regional and global circulation of reproductive gametes (ova, sperm) brings stratification into sharp relief. "Even the reproductive body parts—the ova, sperm and embryos—are stratified and marketed according to their place of origin, the characteristics of their donors, and gender" (Whittaker and Speier 2010:365). The IVF Holiday website claims, "The doctors who interview the donors accept only intelligent and attractive donors." Medical travel intensifies the global stratification of reproduction (Ginsburg and Rapp 1995a). Nahman writes, for example, that the "global economy of eggs means that Jewish Canadian grads get more money than Romanian women" when donating their eggs (2013:31).

The legislative framework of reproductive medicine in the Czech Republic allows for the anonymity of gamete donation, which is a central component of Czech success in cross-border reproductive care.[2] Couples face layers of concern when considering IVF with an egg donor. Questions arise such as whether they want an "open" or "closed" (i.e., anonymous) donation and whether they plan on telling their child that he or she was born of egg donation. This issue becomes more complex if couples cannot give their child any information about the donor.

Czech doctors and nurses have become savvy experts at providing a patient-centered approach to fertility-challenged outsiders. As we will see, Czech clinicians assume the "intimate labor" (Boris and Parreñas 2010) of North Americans. Intimate labor is a lens used to examine the ways private clinics must be nurturing while earning a profit. Like the IVF brokers introduced earlier, clinicians use affective discourse with their clients, since care is a central component of fertility holidays. Reproductive travelers who paint North American doctors as ruthless profit seekers consider Czech doctors substantially different. The affective discourse utilized by brokers and clinics colors patient perceptions of Czech medical care, such that lower costs are interpreted as altruism. As a neoliberal model of health care makes its way across postsocialist Central Europe, it is cloaked and invisible to many North Americans.

Explosion of Czech Reproductive Medicine

Given a rapidly aging European population and a declining birthrate, the Czech government insures up to three cycles of IVF for married Czech women under the age of thirty. "Western civilization depends on IVF," a Czech doctor I interviewed proudly proclaimed. In response to this beckoning call, the Czech Republic has witnessed an explosion of fertility clinics all over the country. Over the past three years, the number of fertility clinics has grown from twenty-five to forty-three, which attests to the high level of demand for ARTs not only at home but also from many other countries. An estimated 20,000 IVF cycles were completed in 2006, a quarter of which were for foreign couples. The mostly private clinics are scattered across the nation. Some are nestled in border towns or situated in urban centers, while others appear in university towns with easy access to student donors. Various clinics may work in tandem via networks, and some clinics share labs.[3] Two clinics have strong connections to the North American brokers IVF Holiday and IVF Choices, in addition to participating in international networks between doctors, brokers, and clinics in Italy, Israel, Germany, and Switzerland.

Czech clinics are a manifestation of "global bio-medical techno-culture with similar clinical procedures, routines, roles, and technology" as clinics in the United States (Speier 2012:219). Daniel, the marketing specialist for IVF Europe, has been a key informant for me over the course of my research. A tall, distinguished, older gentleman, he used to work for pharmaceutical companies before he began promoting Czech reproductive medicine abroad. Multilingual, he maintains the website for IVF Europe, a large network of five fertility clinics that includes the two clinics (CRM and Reprofit) that treat North Americans. Clinics opt to be members of the network to facilitate communication, lower the price of equipment, and strengthen their negotiating power with the Czech government. Because the clinics that constitute IVF Europe complete up to 40 percent of all Czech IVF cycles, they have a strong presence in the country.

Ladislav Pilka opened the Reprofit clinic in 1996 in Brno, the second-largest city in the Czech Republic. Staffed by two doctors, two nurses, and one embryologist, it had grown over the course of fifteen years and had a total of thirty-five employees by 2010. As I was finishing my research in the Czech Republic in 2011, Dr. M. of the clinic told me in his staccato voice they had just hired a seventh doctor, who was proficient in English and Italian. Reprofit has treated foreigners from the very beginning, though it took a decade for North Americans to start coming. Reprofit is a relatively large, bustling clinic that ranked third in the number of total IVF cycles in the Czech Republic in 2011. Seventy percent of the patients at Reprofit are foreign, and roughly 30 percent of these foreign patients are North Americans seeking an egg donor. Most Czech clinics cater to both Czech and foreign clients. Dr. M. estimates that the majority of Czech clinics treat only 20 percent foreign patients, whereas 90 percent of the eggs at Reprofit go to its foreign patients. With such reliance on a donor egg program, Czech clinics must ensure that their supply does not dwindle. Reprofit doubled its donor pool by working with a donor agency in Ostrava. Donors are typically young mothers or university students between the ages of eighteen and twenty-five. Clinics must keep records of their donors for thirty years.

In 2000, Dr. R., who had been mentored by the well-known Pilka at the university in Brno and had been a co-owner of Reprofit, opened his own small clinic in the neighboring town of Zlín. Pilka also invested in this clinic (named CRM), which began with six employees. The new clinic was nevertheless doing 400 cycles a year by its second year, and in 2005, it began treating North American patients. The clinic sits atop a hill nestled among large pine trees, overlooking the entire town, in an old building that belonged to the industrialist Tomáš Baťa (who practically built the town of Zlín to house his shoe manufacturers). The clinic is situated on the second and third floors of the renovated building with the old, creaky elevator that Kay described as rickety.

During the time of my research, North American patients mainly visited these two clinics that were linked to the IVF brokers. The owners of IVF Holiday and IVF Choices had had successful cycles at their respective clinics. Dr. R. describes the history of his association with IVF Holiday:

> Hana has twins from our clinic, daughters, and she told me, "I want to cooperate." I think it's a fairy tale; a lot of people like [Hana] were here who would like to cooperate: from U.S., from Great Britain, from Ireland, and nothing. I think it was nothing too, but Hana is very clever and started this website and after three months, every month, approximately five to ten clients from United States. And after a few first deliveries in the United States, we started to be very popular. Now we have approximately forty to fifty clients every month from all over the world.

When North Americans began visiting the Czech Republic for IVF, one physician, Dr. E., quickly became a favorite of patients despite (or perhaps because of) his broken English. A third of CRM's patients are foreign. The clinic estimates that the numbers of patients it treats each year will only grow.

The clinic in Zlín is well off the beaten tourist path, and patients must travel by car, train, or bus from the Prague airport to get to this hard-to-reach small town. The IVF brokers are affiliated with these distant clinics because they are near their natal homes, and the brokers market smaller towns as part of the appeal for couples to have a less stressful IVF cycle. Patients often claim that they chose to travel to Zlín rather than Prague or Brno because it is "smaller, friendlier." John, a husband from Dallas, also said, "The whole cycle thing is going to be tough, so why not go somewhere where one doesn't have all the everyday stress?" Couples often contrasted their "normal busy" lives with the quiet, relaxing town of Zlín. Patients also assume that because the town is smaller, and the clinic is privately owned, the doctors are more attentive and caring. Petra, owner of IVF Choices, says her patients like "the clinic that is more personal; it is smaller, family-oriented; the owners are the treating doctors."

Increasingly, however, business entrepreneurs are seeking a piece of the reproductive tourism pie. During both summers I spent in the Czech Republic, I tried to speak with doctors at the clinics. In Brno, I spoke only briefly with Dr. M., the head doctor for North American patients. Disarmingly handsome, Dr. M. spoke rapidly, and his body language intimated he had more important things to do. In 2011, he spoke derisively of how yet another clinic was opening up in Brno: "I think until three years ago all the clinics were owned by the doctors. Now I think they are some people who just want to invest. They think this is good market for businessman. But if you don't have a good doctor, there's a lack of doctors. So if you think just invest the money, it's not good. I don't think it will work." The Czech market may have reached a saturation point, or the country may witness an influx of doctors from outside the country.

Fuzzy Legalities

The Czech reproductive tourism industry is growing because of its low price structure and liberal legislation. Unlike its Catholic neighbors Slovakia and Poland, the Czech Republic is predominantly atheist. Given the Catholic Church's strong influence over state regulations of assisted reproductive technologies, the relative lack of strong religious conviction in the Czech Republic allows for looser regulatory frameworks regarding ARTs. In June 2006, the Czech Republic passed legislation that governs sperm and oocyte donation. Under this legislation, donation is legal but must be voluntary, free, and anonymous. Donors cannot be paid directly for their eggs, but they are instead offered attractive "compensatory payments" for the discomfort involved in ovarian stimulation and egg retrieval. In a region where the average monthly salary was under 25,000 crowns (US$1,250) in 2011, donors receive roughly US$1,400 per egg donation. People have argued that in the case of gamete donation, without payment, there would simply not be any donors (Knoll 2012:277). Although they are fairly liberal, Czech clinics will treat only heterosexual, married couples. Only one of my North American informants was openly single, and she had traveled to the Czech Republic for several cycles of IVF. It was clear that Czech clinics were more lenient in ignoring regulations when treating foreign patients, while being adamantly strict about not treating single Czech women (personal communication, Lenka Slepičková July 9, 2014).

One indicator of destination sites of reproductive travel is the availability of certain procedures such as preimplantation genetic diagnosis or surrogacy in addition to gamete donation. A fairly recent technology, PGD is used to diagnose embryos for certain genetic diseases, and it can also be used to select the sex of embryos (a use that is outlawed in the Czech Republic). According to Throsby, "PGD remains highly controversial because of the difficulties of legislating which particular disorders can be legitimately selected out, and the problem of defining what constitutes a disorder in the first place" (2004:12).

The IVF broker Petra drove me to her home village in Moravia in 2010, two months after she had hosted me in her Atlanta home. During our ride, I tried to find out whether or not PGD or surrogacy was practiced in the Czech Republic, since I kept getting evasive or contradictory answers from Czech clinicians (and since I also knew Petra had used a surrogate). Knoll, working with Hungarian fertility clinics, also noted that "regulations" were often contradictory and paradoxical (2012:276). Petra only implied that, because you do not need a medical reason for PGD, there were ways to evade the law:

> The law is that you don't have to have a specific reason to do PGD; it can be that you are trying to get pregnant. We had PGD our first IVF, not for gender selection but for the fact that I have miscarried. We just wanted to make sure that since we are going through the hassle, to see if there is any genetic abnormality. We never asked to know the sex, because that's not important to us. We just wanted to know if there was anything abnormal. But as a result of the PGD, you know the sex.

Both PGD and surrogacy fall within a gray, middle zone. Knoll even admits, regarding the confusion in Hungary: "It is a delicate, often confusing, and sometimes even discouraging matter to do ethnographic fieldwork on the shifting and blurred boundaries between legality and illegality" (2012:281). Doctors often dismissed my questions regarding surrogacy with vague answers. One doctor from a northern clinic in Bohemia first claimed that the surrogacy law is not clear. When I pressed the doctor further, he refused to discuss it, saying, "I will not talk about it because we don't do it and I'm not interested in that."

During the first summer of my research, I was unable to gain access to doctors at the Zlín clinic. Hana had put me in contact with Lenka, the clinic's main coordinator and the wife of Dr. C. Like many Czech and Slovak women, she was extremely petite. As we sat in the conference room, she prepared cappuccinos and told me, "Surrogacy is allowed for Czech clients, not for foreigners. I would say that it's not allowed, but it's not forbidden." Another doctor said that the law was "in process," but not yet complete. However, Dr. V. anticipated its future reality, saying that the medical ability exists, but not the legal structures: "So this is probably not so forbidden to do the surrogacy here, but it is difficult to arrange the adoption process which comes thereafter." Under Czech law, the woman who gives birth to a child is the mother. Hence, if a Czech woman uses a surrogate, she will have to obtain legal papers of adoption from the birth mother once the child is born. Another doctor simply said that they could do it technologically, but that legally "it's on the border." Crossing borders (legal and geographic) is what foreigners will continue to do if surrogacy does become legal. Surrogacy in all its "gray" areas is in a process of review. As a good portion of Czech doctors are urging legal clarity, the practice currently stands ambiguously between technological feasibility and adoption law.

The issue of surrogacy is still being debated in the Czech Republic. In Zlín, Dr. R. and Lenka opposed the provision of surrogacy to foreign couples by implying that the uncomfortable association of babies and money becomes overt in cases of surrogacy. Lenka referred to surrogacy as "business with children." This distinction between surrogacy and egg donation by some working in Czech clinics is fascinating. Interestingly, the famous Dr. Pilka, whose name is associated with both clinics, advocated the legalization of surrogacy. Dr. M. in Brno currently serves on a committee overseeing the possibility of a surrogacy law, and he claims there is an equal division between those for and against permitting surrogacy.

"Closed" Egg Donation

Despite the confusion surrounding surrogacy, Czech clinics do market themselves to patients seeking ovum donation. Clinic websites advertise in English, German, Italian, and Russian, and the advertisements stress the ready availability of student ova donors with only a three-month waiting period. Czech clinics assure potential reproductive travelers of a ready supply of Czech eggs. Advertisements for egg donors adorn bulletin boards of university campuses and trams, and some clinics recruit donors through regional radio stations. In addition, egg donors tell friends and family about donation. Ob-gyn offices may refer not just patients but also potential donors.

Besides university students, many egg donors are young mothers. I was told that Czech women should donate only three times, yet there are no regulatory frameworks to enforce this rule. Lenka admitted that Czech women donate their eggs for the money. There was no squeamishness in saying this was their motivation, and she explained that Czech donors clearly distinguish between an egg and a child. Lenka bluntly said to me, "I never met [a] donor who would do that from my point of view from just altruistic reasons. It is all about money, and they are not as sensitive as I should say they should be . . . they just ask when they get the money. That's why I don't think that they really realize what they are doing." While critics tend to denounce the financial motivations of egg donors, students tend to have a bit more leeway if they are financially motivated, since the money is supposedly going toward their education (Almeling 2006:153).

The clinic in Zlín has 500 women who are potential egg donors, which, according to Lenka, is more than they need. Lenka explains how the clinic categorizes its donors: "A is perfect, pass, more than average, B is average, and C is not very good . . . and because we have so many donors, we really do not have a need. They are in the database. We have some Cs, but I do not have a need to call her because I still have enough As and Bs." Women often call the clinic to inquire about the possibility of donating their eggs. As in the case of North America, there is an "oversupply of women willing to be egg donors . . . far outstripping recipient demand. Despite this abundance, egg donor fees hold steady and are often calibrated by staff perceptions of a woman's characteristics and a recipient's wealth" (Almeling 2007:336).

North Americans often wonder aloud about the stark price difference between IVF in the Czech Republic and in the United States, but they do not focus on the fact that Czech egg donors are paid significantly less than North Americans. Waldby and Mitchell, among others, have shown how "a transfer of tissues from one person to another follows the trajectories of power and wealth, as the poor sell their body parts to those with more wealth" (2006:8). These authors complicate the dichotomy of framing human tissue donation as either a gift or a commodity system. Such a dichotomy fails to take into account "the political economy of the modern world of globalized biotechnology" (9). In fact, "gift and commodity systems interpenetrate each other in increasingly complex ways" (25). Like human tissue, egg donation is both gift and commodity exchange, signaling an overlap as with the intimate labor provided by actors in the tourism industry.

The Czech Republic is unusual in that egg and sperm donation are anonymous, or "closed." A couple cannot peruse photographs of potential donors, and their child will never have access to the donor's identity. Anonymity is meant to protect the privacy of both the donor and the recipient. Hertz has suggested that many single North Americans choose anonymous donation in order to avoid legal risk (2006:x). In addition, anonymous donation reaffirms broader cultural values of anonymity and privacy prevalent in North America (Hertz 2006:65). Early phases of reproductive technology debates claimed anonymity was "needed to protect the nuclear family, saving it equally from intrusive strangers and the shadow of incest" (Strathern 2005:31).

Dr. S. had acted as a reproductive specialist for IVF broker Petra in North America. He was the first doctor I spoke with during my research about reproductive tourism. He claimed that anonymous donation protects both parties: "The anonymity piece is really about the parent. It's about keeping the parent from being a pain in the butt, and harassing the donor. And it's about the donor not harassing the parent." Most Czech doctors I spoke with were unwavering in their claim that anonymous donation is the best. Anonymous egg donation is called "closed," whereas donor programs in other parts of the world are "open." However, debates have come full circle to a discussion of a child's right to knowledge of his or her own genetic identity (Strathern 2005:31). Scholars have written about the ways that human tissues often have "affective significance" in that they can often "represent complex ideas about human identity and community" (Waldby and Mitchell 2006:6).

I finally gained access to Dr. R. during my second summer of research. Dr. R. is the owner of the clinic in Zlín, and he was very warm, offering his undivided attention for several hours (unlike Dr. M., who rushed me through our brief interviews both summers). At the time of our conversation, Dr. R.'s wife was writing her master's thesis on the issue of donation. Dr. R. even labeled the two different "open" and "closed" philosophies of donation as American and European. He claimed that many North Americans actually prefer "open" donation so they can meet the egg donor, know more about her, and have a chance to thank her with a small gift. According to Dr. R., Europeans are not interested in disclosing to their children that they are from egg donation, whereas North Americans generally do plan to disclose. Dr. R. said that he was not sure which approach was best, and he was also thinking of ways to meet the North American demand for "open" donation in the future. He knew the clinic had lost potential clients who sought open donation, and he was therefore seeking ways to increase his client base.

Despite his claim that Europeans prefer anonymous donation, there has been a general legal trend in Europe to discourage it. Austria and Germany have recently passed legislation that ensures children born of gamete donation have access to the donor's identity once they are eighteen years old. There is a nagging suspicion among Czech doctors that if they followed this European trend, their segment of the market for fertility travel would crumble. The Czech Republic is treating not only North Americans but also Irish, British, Austrian, German, Polish, Russian, and Scandinavian patients. Doctors are literally banking on the fact that the law will remain the same with the current government. Dr. R. worried: "I don't know. . . . But if [donation] will be open, children in the future have the possibility to know [their] donor, it will be problem." Dr. M. bluntly concurred, saying, "We are done" if a new Czech law stipulates that donation must be open. He claimed patients would simply continue traveling farther east to places where anonymity is assured.

Tom and Hana promote the anonymity of egg donation as part of their marketed fertility holidays. Tom assumed it would be a strong selling point for North Americans who already face the stigma of infertility. For many couples who reach the point of needing IVF with egg donation, the secrecy that envelops their struggle with infertility often thickens. The desire for discretion for those who are seeking IVF using egg donation has been documented (Inhorn 2003). Women who need IVF with an egg donor may also need to conduct some "ontological choreography," a term that captures the multifaceted struggles patients face when confronting possibilities offered by ARTs (C. Thompson 2005). While some couples may admit to using IVF, they may not tell people about the fact that they are using an egg donor for fear of further stigma. Tom of IVF Holiday intimated, "Women are happy that it's an anonymous donor. You don't want to have to worry about someone knocking on your door. They can feel comfortable being in the no-tell camp, knowing that the donor doesn't even know if there is a birth, and the only thing she knows about them is that they exist. They don't know where you're from, they don't know how old you are. You exist. There's a woman out there who wants your eggs, and that's all they know and that's all they ever know." In fact, most egg donors are unaware that their eggs are donated to foreign clients. I asked Dr. M. if Czech egg donors know the number of foreign couples coming to the clinic for egg donation. He claimed that possibly half of them know. However, because donation is anonymous, he is not at liberty to share with them any information. Dr. M. said that those egg donors who do know are usually happy that their eggs were given to a foreign couple, since this lessens the chance of children with the same genetic makeup meeting. Jana, one of Petra's Czech-based coordinators, assumed that most donors do not know their eggs are going to foreign couples, but she also claimed they probably do not care.

While anonymous gamete donation is assumed to ensure a larger pool of donors, not all North American recipients necessarily opted to travel to the Czech Republic for the anonymity. Suzanne had been one of my survey respondents through Petra's IVF Choices, and we first spoke over the phone in the fall of 2010. She had plenty of time on her hands, since she was on strict bed rest. I met Suzanne, a Canadian doctor, in person when I was in Montreal for a national conference a few years later. We sipped cappuccinos as light snowflakes descended upon the city in November. Suzanne had had one "open donation" cycle of IVF in Canada. Open donation is mandatory in Canada. Unfortunately, her donor had suffered hyperstimulated ovaries (the most common painful side effect of taking fertility medication to stimulate a higher egg production). Given the trouble her donor had faced and the difficulty of finding willing donors, Suzanne opted to travel to the Czech Republic, even though she preferred open donation. She now worries about not being able to give her child information about the genetic mother.[4] Indeed, "The politics of anonymous donor–assisted families do not allow women to answer these fundamental questions of identity for their children" (Hertz 2006:61).

Just as couples and women who undergo IVF with an egg donor must weigh the issue of having a "closed" donation when shopping for clinics, they need to decide what characteristics are important in selecting a donor. As consumers working within a closed system, they are more restricted because of the anonymity of donation. However, couples can request things like a particular eye color, hair color, or blood type. A doctor in Prague hypothesized: "I think those which are so much concerned about eye color, blood type, they don't want to tell in the future." Those couples that do plan to tell do not need to be so concerned about the donor type strictly matching. Similarly, Lenka from the Zlín clinic divided recipients into two categories: those who only want a healthy child and those who have "crazy" parameters. She estimated that 50 percent want to create "princesses," a term that evokes notions of a perfect child.

Czech hosts describe North Americans as "choosy" about the details of their donor. Given the lack of regulation in North America regarding gamete donation, at home patients can opt for open or closed donation. This may cause them to be more demanding. Petra even disparaged some clients:

> I would say that Americans are very needy and demanding when it comes to egg donation. People from the other countries are just grateful for the opportunity, and Americans demand round face, pointy nose, hair to be wavy but not too curly, just very picky and demanding. It's because it is possible here [in the United States] to get the whole profile of the donor, but that's what you pay $40,000 for. We cannot provide you that. An anonymous donor, if you choose that option, gets more narrow, you can't be that picky about it.

At issue here seems to be a general critique of the neoliberal framework of reproductive medicine. The economic reality of reproductive medicine as a private business begets patients who are consumers and therefore want choices.

Restrictions have in fact tightened over the past few years in response to North American "choosiness." When IVF Holiday first began sending clients to the Czech Republic, Hana would simply call Dr. R. and (for example) informally ask him for a musically inclined donor. Patients I met in later years complained that they received little to no information about their donor. Leah also noted a shift from her first visit to the Czech Republic to her third. She said that recipients do not receive information about the donor until they have already begun medication. She was not sure why the shift had occurred, but it constrained recipients, who could not really back out after beginning medication. Similarly, Dr. M., who used to give patients a choice, admitted to stopping when he found them to be too demanding. The gatekeepers of information about donors are tightening and formalizing regulations about information that is passed on to recipients, narrowing the amount of knowledge shared.

Intimate Labor of Brokers

Juan and Anita had used the services of IVF Holiday for their two trips to Zlín. They were picked up at the airport and then driven to their accommodations in Zlín and to the clinic. For couples who had never been to the Czech Republic, this door-to-door service provided by IVF brokers was reassuring and calming. They compared brokers to travel agents who arranged transportation and translation.

Maria—who had traveled to the Czech Republic for IVF a total of three times, and who brought her husband and three children with her—goes so far as to claim that Hana and Tom do not even care about profit and that the brokerage is purely altruistic: "It is nice because you know that they're doing it to help other people have families. It's not their supporting income, they have a lot of other things that they do. It's nice to know that they're not there to just rape my wallet." This personal, attentive treatment provided by IVF brokers is of the utmost importance in giving clients the sense that they care. Allan and Alida, the Austin couple who cooked their own breakfast, spoke repeatedly about Tom and Hana's excellent care. They had worked with Tom, who was their main contact for IVF Holiday. Allan kept saying, "I would recommend Tom the broker, because he's got his family member over there." As Allan saw it, "just being able to pick up the phone any time of day and being able to call" while in the Czech Republic was the most valued service. Tom and Hana told clients to call them (on the mobile phone they provide) any time they needed translation assistance or had a question. This meant that Tom and Hana's phone rang off the hook at all hours of the night.

I heard the same story from both Julie in South Carolina and Faith in Georgia about a train adventure they had during their first trip. There were frequent narratives about confusing train travel, and even anthropologists are at risk of boarding the wrong train or not getting off at the right juncture. Both women told me how they phoned Hana and Tom whenever they needed assistance. Julie remembered: "We even called them in the middle of the night, when we were on our way to Poland and about to be kicked off the train because we hadn't bought the right tickets, and the guy didn't speak any language we knew. So we called them, in the middle of the night, and [Hana] helped the guy figure out what we needed to do so we wouldn't get kicked off the train in the middle of nowhere." Calling someone late at night evokes phoning parents during an emergency. The labor of IVF brokers is intimate, demanding, and time-consuming, and the brokers must always be accessible to the clients who have trusted them and traveled halfway across the world under their guidance and protection. This intimate labor is radically different from feeling like a number in U.S. fertility clinics.

Andrea Whittaker has posed the following question with regard to cross-border reproductive care: "At what critical junctures in the experience do local cultures, values, practices, histories and regulations intrude upon these technological zones?" (2008:285). In the case of reproductive travel to the Czech Republic, the IVF broker coordinates these critical junctures at the clinic. In addition to making travel arrangements, Hana and Petra are cultural brokers. Having lived in the United States for nearly a decade, these women are travel-savvy about the Czech Republic, yet they can also anticipate the needs of North Americans. Hana and Petra are well versed in anticipating a North American vision of Czech culture. In fact, Hana was very skilled at feigning surprise at Czech customs. She often met with her clients when she was in town. I joined Hana, Alison (my good friend from Minnesota), and Alison's sister for lunch one afternoon in late June 2011. I noted how often Hana steered the conversation toward talk about strange toilets, bathroom doors, foods, and customs.

The cultural and clinical meeting of North Americans and Czechs is eased as IVF brokers "coordinate" these encounters. They warn patients about the oddities in the clinic. Like travel brochures and guidebooks that prepare tourists for their destination by presenting certain "narratives" (Urry 2002), broker websites offer images of Czech clinics for patients to consume. Hence, patients feel well prepared when they recognize the clinic immediately upon arrival. Brokers also arm clients with knowledge to help them maneuver through a foreign clinic. North Americans traveling to the Czech Republic are typically well versed in the world of ARTs, yet their entrance into the Czech clinic still needs to be managed.

Nearly all of my informants at one point related a funny anecdote about their experience of nudity at the Czech clinic. Knowing they lacked a liberal attitude toward the body, Hana warned her clients to wear a dress or skirt. Patients often told me they appreciated the "warning" provided by Hana. As Jessica remembers,

> You know for all the moments that are slightly awkward, that are different from the States, Hana kind of warned us, which is another thing I liked about going through them. They warned us, "You get this wrap kind of thing," which is weird having an ultrasound and you don't have that here (pointing to her lower body). So she told us to wear a skirt and then you won't be panicked and naked, even though the doctor probably doesn't care, it's awkward for you. I'm glad that she forewarned us, because I've just worn a skirt to every appointment and I've been fine. So for those kinds of things I felt prepared by IVF Holiday for some of the potentially awkward moments.

In warning North American patients about possible nudity at the clinic, IVF brokers are coordinating potentially disruptive clinical experiences. As Becker notes, "Examining NRTs [new reproductive technologies] globally is one route to understanding the global landscape and intertwining of cultures through technology" (2000:249). The IVF brokers address possible instances of discomfort due to different clinical procedures in addition to arranging medical protocols and travel itineraries. The fact that this topic of conversation kept surfacing bears witness to the importance of clinical coordination enacted by IVF brokers.

Choosing White Babies

Three-quarters of North Americans traveling to the Czech Republic for fertility procedures are seeking IVF with egg donation, based on estimates given to me by IVF brokers and Czech doctors. Others (Nahman 2013) have written about the preference for a white child, and North Americans traveling to the Czech Republic are unabashedly open about their preference (often cloaked by the claim that they want a child who "resembles them").

In North America, notions of ethnicity and race are often used interchangeably. Furthermore, ideas of race also pervade notions of nationality, despite the fact that the United States is a multiethnic nation. I was visiting with the owner and main receptionist of a hotel in Prague where I had spent a month during the summer of 2012 with students. They were inquiring about my recent move to Texas and laughing as they told me about a couple from Texas who had stayed at their hotel. Petr, the tall, lanky receptionist, humorously told me about how the couple resembled one another, their bodies shaped like bowling balls. He was blown away when the woman had asked for a Coke with breakfast. But he saved the funniest anecdote for last, recalling how on the section of the registration card that asked for their nationality, the couple had written, in capital letters: WHITE.

Linda and Michael were from Seattle, and they were giddy with excitement when I met them immediately after their embryo transfer. Linda wanted to talk in their apartment so that she could prop herself up in bed as Michael tenderly cared for her by bringing juice, pillows, and anything else she desired. They were very active and loved hiking around the town. Young for their age—Linda was forty and Michael was sixty—they were obviously in love as a newly married couple and kept track of how many months they had been together. Linda said, "We wanted Caucasian ancestry. I didn't do a lot of research, but I did look into going to India, South Africa, but I really didn't spend a lot of time because if we were going to adopt somebody of a different ethnicity that was fine, but if we had the choice we wanted to have a Caucasian child." The overwhelming majority (95 percent) of the North Americans headed to the Czech Republic are white, though I did meet one Puerto Rican couple. Ben and Claudia were a mixed-race couple, so I found it intriguing when Ben, a black man, also stated the preference for a white donor: "We wanted Claudia to be part of the equation, that they could match her. So Central Europe was a good choice, the northern European countries were a choice. Spain you do get some *blancos* there, but it's hard to find her profile match with the donor window that we're looking in." In reproductive tourism, gametes are "culturally charged; they carry ethnic, caste and racial value" (Bharadwaj 2008, cited in Whittaker and Speier 2010:378).

There are racialized notions of Europe at work when couples choose a destination for IVF. Based on these understandings, couples rule out certain destinations when shopping for fertility holiday destinations. Faith had said, "I wasn't really interested in going to . . . what I considered a Third World country." Daniel had concerns about going to Mexico, even if it was much closer to their home in Los Angeles than the Czech Republic, since he wanted a donor who resembled his wife, Maureen. Valerie talked about ruling out Spain: "I looked at different websites for Greece and Spain. We talked about the fact where Spain they're gonna be really, really dark for the most part. I didn't want this super-brown baby, because he's pretty pale, he's got blond hair, blue eyes. I'm Italian and I do get pretty tan, but I'm not that dark naturally. And that would be too . . . I don't want it. None of my friends know we're doing donor egg. I'm not telling." Dr. M. of the Brno clinic said most South Americans tend to go to Spain; North Americans tend to go to the Czech Republic. A couple's skin color determines their travel route for fertility care. Couples choose the Czech Republic for white egg donors, for ones who will resemble them. The Czech Republic's population is fairly ethnically homogeneous, and Roma and Vietnamese constitute a very small minority. Egg donors are primarily "white" in the sense used by North Americans and Czechs.

Concerns about any connection between creating a baby and the marketplace begin to emerge more starkly when couples pursue IVF using an egg donor. Juan had read somewhere that using an egg donor was the equivalent of shopping, which he found unsettling. He admitted, "We read somewhere they made fun of it, like you were shopping in a store. I don't look at it like that, but when they put it out there like that, it kind of feels like that." Another blog entry written by a North American reproductive traveler was entitled "Going Gattaca," evoking a futuristic, eugenically minded society. These instances reflect general discomfort in using an egg donor or acknowledging the economic element of having a child via reproductive technologies. Just as Americans who have adopted abroad have little to say about "the moral aspects of using their status and resources as consumers to take children from choiceless 'surrendering' mothers," North Americans do not speak to the global inequalities that frame reproductive tourism (Solinger 2002:29). Of course, most tourists do not speak to global inequalities more generally when they travel abroad.

In the United States, genetics plays a weighty role in how people conceptualize their future children, in both a behavioral and a physical sense. There is also a notion that the child is half of each parent. Valerie worried: "What if it doesn't look like me? It's been tough for me, because it's not gonna be mine, my genetics. But at this point I don't care. I wanna have a baby. We have his . . . hopefully they get all the good qualities, and I wanted to make sure that we had a really good donor." Couples often imagine or hope that the husband and all of his "good" parts may be passed on. Couples choose to travel to the Czech Republic claiming they want an egg donor with phenotypical similarities. Nash has written about "cultures of relatedness" to characterize Irish Americans tracing their ancestral roots back to Ireland. She argues that such actors perform and produce the practice of genealogy (2003:181). Such cultures of relatedness are global and diasporic, with social and political roots. Similarly, reproductive travelers are engaged in creating and sustaining geographies of relatedness that "both depend on and displace the significance of blood relations" (181).

Dr. M. said of the North Americans: "All of them are the same: they want to have a baby that looks like them. This is the truth. Eighty percent are very interested in the physical features, 10 percent are not interested at all, but they want to have a baby, and 10 percent just want something. But a lot of people want the copy." During the summer of

2011, I traveled to Spain, which boasts a much larger reproductive travel industry than the Czech Republic. Dr. O. was generous and willing to speak with me at his Barcelona clinic. He told me that he spends a lot of time talking with his clients about resemblance: "You spend a lot of time discussing the phenotype and how important is it. I usually tell my patients I just made them a piece of clay and the hard job starts when they deliver, because they have to shape that piece of clay. I'm gonna do my best to give them the best piece of clay that I can, but there is a lot to be done after that." In saying this, Dr. O. tries to minimize his patients' stress about resemblance.

Matching an egg donor with a recipient is, according to a Prague doctor, "subject to feeling." It is not an exact science. "Matching" occurs on a phenotypical level. North Americans want a child who will resemble them, in addition to having particular characteristics. Some North Americans I met wanted a donor who was intelligent, which they equated with a university-level education. Some couples preferred an egg donor who was still attending the university. Alison, on the other hand, believed that education level was culturally determined and therefore not important. Generally, doctors can match easily with clear criteria like education level or blood type.

Even those who do not indicate a preference for some kind of matching generally do want assurances that the egg donor is young (which indicates the viability of her eggs) or is a proven donor. Suzanne, the Canadian doctor, explained this preference:

> We could be as picky as we wanted. So we just said all that matters to us was that she be as young as possible with previous successful donation or previous successful pregnancy. Preferably that she be in college, and that was it. And I sent them a photo of myself, because they said they would try to match my characteristics. But I told them that that was much less important to me than her being young, because I know the most important determinants for success are age of donor and previous success. So that was more important to us than anything else.

Many women I spoke to commended Lenka at the Zlín clinic for having a good reputation as a "matchmaker" between egg donors and recipients.[5] Leah acknowledged the level of trust being given to the clinic:

"Apparently she's very good at it. Apparently. I mean how can people know? But there's a lot of trust in them to choose."

Angela, whose father had been a university professor, was the most cynical North American I met over the course of my research. Her sharp wit often had me laughing. She told me how she kept telling Tom, the broker, her biggest fear before her trip. She said to him, "I don't want a Marty Feldman baby." Her husband was shocked when I expressed my ignorance about who Marty Feldman was, and they described a man with unusual features who is famous for playing hunchback characters and monsters in films. Angela continued:

> That's my only fear, is that the doctors over there are rubbing their hands together going, "Ah these naive Americans, here comes another one." Bring in Helga with the crazy eyeballs, "Let me drop the egg, OK here comes the sperm. Very good, we have another one now" . . . I'm like, "What am I doing?" That's what I said to Chris [her husband], "What am I doing?" Going to this country, I've never been there, I know no one, and I'm just trusting unknown people to pick some random woman's eggs that I'm going to allow to just like be put inside my body with my husband's sperm. Ah, it's so weird.

Angela could only reconcile herself with egg donation if there was a resemblance: "If I'm going to be carrying this baby, I think it would feel a little better if I knew there was some kind of resemblance. Sorry." The fear of a "Marty Feldman baby" reveals the stress and angst involved in placing one's trust in a foreign clinic to handle such intimate details.

While some women struggle with accepting the idea of an egg donor, others readily embrace this option, revealing their ambivalence about their own genetic makeup. Maureen was emphatic that she did not want to pass on hereditary diseases that occur in her family, while her husband, Daniel, felt he should pass on traits. He explained: "At the same time, I felt I could add some good genes to the family. I felt there was something to pass on. When Maureen started looking in Europe, my donor egg concerns became less apparent, because I knew in the Czech Republic . . . we could find eggs of someone that is tall, light skinned, blue eyes." As Rothman writes of adoption as "freeing" for couples who do not want to pass on "bad genes" (2005:66), the same can be said for women like Maureen. Couples who opt for IVF with an egg donor are still concerned with having a genetic link between one parent and the child. Alida explained, "With IVF it's at least half the equation. It's your genes and you know that that you can control certain characteristics of what you want. We want a five foot five, brown haired, blue-eyed, Czech student at twenty-four years old who doesn't smoke and isn't too hairy."

A common circulating myth I heard while speaking with several couples in the Czech Republic was the possible meeting between donor and recipient in the clinic. Several women wondered aloud whether or not they were there at the same time, or even claimed they spotted a woman who was surely their donor. This topic was often discussed in whispers over breakfast. Cindy explained her thoughts as she sat at the clinic for her first appointment (which was also the day that she and I first met at the clinic). She said: "I thought it was just odd that it looked like it was donors sitting with the recipients.[6] The lady sitting next to Scott was younger, by herself. So I was very curious in my brain. I look around thinking, 'Could it be her? Was she one of them?' Or even, I saw another girl, so that just makes you wonder." Interestingly, she immediately categorized Czech women in the waiting room as donors rather than fellow patients. I asked Ludmilla, a Czech coordinator in Zlín, whether donors and recipients were in fact at the clinic at the same time. She replied: "Yes, but they don't know about it. When the donor comes here they come early in the morning, and they are at the waiting room, or after the surgery room. The day the male partner has to come for a sperm contribution in the morning, but they are in the front of the same floor. They don't meet together, but they are here at the same time." Maintaining anonymity requires work for the clinic. Clinicians must carefully maneuver timing and spacing of donors and recipients.

Doctors Who Care

Just as IVF brokers provide intimate labor to their clients, clinicians and nurses in the Czech Republic do as well. Patients draw a sharp contrast between their past experiences at home and abroad. The preliminary survey I distributed at the beginning of my research to previous reproductive travelers asked patients about their experiences in the United

States and for their assessment of their treatment in the Czech Republic. Most respondents were unsatisfied with the care and high costs of treatment in North America, and their responses about Czech clinics were often diametrically opposed to these previous negative experiences. Patients claimed that they had been treated as if they were human in the Czech Republic, as opposed to being treated as a wallet or an ATM in North America. More important, in the Czech Republic they felt respected.

Marcia Inhorn argues, "IVF providers have built successful practices based on their technical competence" where doctors provide "patient-centered care" (2003:136). Czech doctors appear attentive to North American patients. One of the first patients I met online was Kay, whose husband was in the military, so they lived overseas. Kay was critical of her treatment in the United States: "I never felt like a patient, just a checkbook. The treatment was never discussed with me; I was just told what to do and when that didn't work, there was no discussion of why; [I was] just told to write another check and come back for cycle day two monitoring." On the other hand, she characterized her Czech doctor as "warm, friendly and truly interested in getting his patients pregnant." I argue that North American patients interpret more affordable care as compassionate care.

I asked all patients I interviewed to describe the main reasons they traveled to the Czech Republic for care. Maria could not limit her answer to one reason:

I know I'm coming to a place where they actually care. They want to see you get pregnant, because their main staple is not from people coming over for IVF. Their main staple is everyone in the Czech Republic who needs IVF gets three IVF treatments on the state. That's their main staple, so they're taken care of. And we come here and we know that they are going to do what's best for us and advise as to what's best for us, not what's best for them, or what fits their schedule. If you need a transfer on a Saturday, they're here. If you call that clinic twenty-four hours a day, seven days a week, somebody's answering the phone. It's just the whole experience for the price is. . . . Honestly, if I had the money, I would have paid twice the amount that we would have paid in the States to have the better experience.

Here, Maria outright refuses to believe or think that Czech doctors are driven by profit motives. This seems to be a glaring blindness or refusal to notice the marketplace of medicine in Central Europe.

As mentioned earlier, Tom and Hana had a successful cycle of IVF at the Zlín clinic. Patients utilize the discourse of gift giving when speaking of fertility clinics. Just as "donated" eggs are deemed gifts with no absolute market value, Hana nostalgically remembered Dr. C. as the doctor who "gave" her children. As I have argued elsewhere, "The language of gift giving concretizes the intimate labor performed by doctors and embryologists and is an externalization of the affective discourse around these commoditized transactions" (Speier 2015).

The nurses and doctors at the clinic knew that many North American clients were lower middle class. They were mindful of this and often suggested ways for patients to save money. Faith, whose husband worked three jobs, remembered Dr. E., who had since left the clinic: "One of their doctors at the time I really loved. He was extremely personable, seemed very caring, tried to help us save money in different ways." Patients often remarked, stunned, how the nurses at the clinic simply handed them bags of expensive medications before they even paid for them. Faith continued, speaking about the respect she received, "I was actually treated with more respect, more like a queen." This respect and care stand in stark contrast to patients' past experiences in American clinics and also evoke the "queen for a day" element of tourism in general. North American patients I spoke with felt empowered in a Czech clinical setting. It is at the Czech clinic that patients become blind to the neoliberal framework of Czech reproductive medicine, by interpreting lower prices as evidence of altruism and not examining the political economic context of reproductive travel. Given currency exchange rates, salary scales, and public investment in health care, services that appear "altruistically cheap" and "humanely available" by U.S. standards actually earn a profit in the Czech context.

Couples I spoke with appreciated that they were never rushed during doctor consultations, and they felt that they had more access to information as well as decision-making power. In fact, Czech doctors were willing to mirror the IVF protocols that couples had previously had in North America. This fact comforted couples. For example, Suzanne (the Canadian doctor) had received her protocol from the Czech clinic but noticed that it was out of sync with what her Canadian clinic had given her. She spoke to the Czech clinic via the broker, and the clinic acceded to her wishes. The patient in this context has the upper hand. As patients become diligent consumers, doctors become entrepreneurial: "The position of the doctors is changing: in a highly capitalized and privatized area they become commercial actors themselves, follow commercial interests, and engage in directly commercial relationships with other doctors, institutes, and with other clients" (Polat 2012:221).

Another important difference was the amount of time that Czech doctors spent in consultation with patients. There was never a sense of impatience. Instead, Czech doctors displayed a willingness to answer any questions. There was a subtle shift in the relationship between doctor and patient in this context. Linda imagined the thoughts of clinicians who always paid close attention to her: "'We understand you don't speak the language. We're going to do the best we can to make you feel comfortable.' All my questions were always answered, and I never felt put off. I never felt like I was being ignored or kind of shoved to the side, which was really nice considering I felt like that when I left my clinic."

Similarly, Lauren and John felt that the Czech doctors were "twice as sensitive" as the doctors they had encountered in Texas. Lauren said of her first Czech clinic that she "felt like we were the most important people in that room." Again, this relaxed atmosphere was often contrasted with the bustling, frantic North American clinics. Valerie from San Diego painted the contrast: "We had to make the doctor wait. So everything is relaxed and mellow. They're explaining in no rush. American doctors—they're pumping you in and out. They don't care if they spend five minutes with you. They're like 'Get out, move on.' They get a little frustrated if you ask too many questions. Where here, he was just very slow and methodical. Granted he has to speak English, but it's like he was just waiting for us to say something." April was surprised that when she walked into the Czech doctor's office, he was already sitting there, waiting. The tables are turned, and patients are empowered. Alison found it strange that the Czech doctor kept asking her what she thought: "They keep asking your opinion. Everything's about what you want to do. They tell you what they think, but not really. She said, 'I see you were on 300 IUs of injectable a day for your last IVF, is it OK if we do that again?' I'm like, 'Well, you tell me.'" While Jenny embraced a strong-willed stance as a patient-consumer, others like Alison and April found this shift slightly unsettling. It is as consumers rather than as patients that some women feel more "dignity, more power" (Rothman 2004:283).

Even further, patients abroad continue to claim empowerment as they become personally responsible for their care. Jenny, the woman who in the last chapter was described as encouraging others to "do the research," urges women to make demands on Czech doctors:

> I really had to just pretty much tell today's doctor—he just wanted me to do their standard protocol—and I said, "It's not happening," I have to actually lay down the law, "No you need to do this." He doesn't understand, but it doesn't matter if he understands. Very few people demand. Most people, even Maureen, who is talking to him, "I'll do whatever you recommend." I would NEVER say that in a million years. Have I ever said that to a doctor? I would never say, "Whatever you recommend."

In her rant, Jenny goes so far as to discredit the Czech doctor's medical authority and knowledge.

Finally, North Americans are struck by the fact that they have access to more information in a Czech clinic. Leah, the blonde Canadian woman whom I had met at the clinic, told me how she had been able to meet with the embryologist. This is something that simply would not happen in North American clinics:

> You actually sit with the embryologist. She actually has on the screen numbers and she'll go through and tell you, "You have x number of embryos with this quality and that quality. How many do you want to transfer?" You can ask them for a recommendation. You actually speak to the embryologist, and they have quite a few there, and they will be frank with you, they will be honest. But you actually get to talk to them. At home, you never see an embryologist. You never ever see one. Here if you were really stressed and you asked, "How are my embryos doing?" I am sure they would tell you. At home you don't hear of anything. So I can actually sit and talk to an embryologist? That's pretty fantastic.

This hints that couples have more access to the "backstage" of Czech clinics and also have more (yet sometimes difficult) decision-making power. There is a sense that North Americans feel cared for and respected because of this. They sense genuine concern and appreciate the attention that is given to them in a calming manner.

Savvy Clinic Ousts IVF Broker

The IVF brokers were necessary in laying the track for the global care chain of reproductive travel between North America and the Czech Republic. However, their role had diminished significantly by the end of my research. I argue that this happened for three reasons: they could not meet the demand; Czech clinics grew savvy in offering patient-centered care; and patient-consumers became activists by encouraging future clients to "do it yourself." In the first few years, as business steadily grew with the births of their first clients' babies, Tom and Hana reached a point (particularly in the summer) when they could not meet all the demand. They looked into working with clinics in Prague, which they decided would have been too expensive. They also looked to Slovakia, where the popular Dr. E. had moved. Six couples went to that clinic, yet it was a failed performance. This gives a glimpse into the necessary conditions for successful reproductive tourism. Hana told me why the Slovakia partnership did not work:

> The doctor in Slovakia was very Slovakian. He was not prepared for Americans at all. People from U.S. want something a little extra when they come. Because they are going out of the U.S., and they know that they are not paying as much as in the U.S. They still think that they should get the same level of care. However, he was not very willing. For example, progesterone is important after about two weeks of the transfer, because that's when the embryos start to do this and that. It's just that the U.S. doctors have in the patient's heads that they need it right away, the level is to be so high. The level gets high if there's pregnancy, and the body naturally increases it. They are like, "I need it high and I need it measured right now. If it's not, I need injections, and I need this and I need that." He was like, "No. That's bull crap, and I'm not going to do this for you." I am like, "Can you just . . . How much does it cost you to do that test? They are willing to pay." He's like, "It's bull crap." I am like, "I know it. You know it. They don't know it. They will not take your word for it. Just take that

twenty bucks and do it if you want to get paid." He's like, "It's not about the money." I'm like, "It's about being a doctor. They want to have this progesterone test done." It was not worth it, turned it into more headache.

This episode reveals the necessary comportment for doctors treating foreign patients. They must acquiesce to patient demands if they want their business. Hana's labeling of the doctor as "Slovakian" hints at his being a more traditional and less entrepreneurial doctor, who insists on ultimate medical authority. This doctor staunchly refused to give an unnecessary test despite the potential earned income. Hana questioned his medical decision making, since she believed the test would cause no harm and would appease her clients. Also, she knew that money always speaks.

As Tom and Hana were looking for additional clinic partners, the Zlín clinic opened its doors to patients directly in March 2009 by hiring its own coordinators. We can understand the clinic coordinator as an example of what Gibbon and Novas identify as "new forms of labour" that are related to new biomedical technologies and understandings of biosociality (2008:10). Hana felt betrayed by the clinic, though she continued to work with it. Clinics began hiring their own coordinators because doctors were finding themselves answering too many direct questions through Hana. In March 2009, Lenka stepped in as the IVF coordinator for English-speaking patients. The wife of Dr. C., Lenka is a petite Slovakian who has traveled extensively throughout the United States. As one who also needed in vitro fertilization for her second child, she is able to empathize with patients and the pain of infertility. Also, she knows the proper greeting of a hug, and will accompany patients into the doctor's consultation. She is quite similar to Hana and Petra in the way she bridges Czech and American cultural differences.

Dr. R., the owner of the Zlín clinic, explained how much of the work of the coordinator occurs online:

I think it's normal if [a woman is] infertile in United States, to look on Internet, "What do I have to do?" One possibility in United States of America, and second abroad, all around the world. I think she sends in one, two days, for example, 50 e-mails, the same e-mails to fifty clinics. I think it's the way and she waits. Fifty e-mails, for example, ten answers . . . let me research and start to look on Internet. "What is your clinic? How does it work? What do I have to do? What is your guarantee—it's very important—what is your guarantee? What I have to pay?" I think she choose[s] one of them. This is work of coordinators, because it's like doctors working with clients, from morning to the afternoon, and it is not possible to write yes we have zoo, park, three hotels, we have four-star hotels. You have a pet? OK, I try to find . . . it is the work of our coordinators. For example, if the client is here for three weeks for all IVF treatment, it's a lot of time, and they want to prepare trips to Vienna, Prague, Bratislava, and it's not work for doctor.

As the number of foreign patients increased, doctors could not handle the demand for various services through IVF Holiday. Thus, the clinic recognized the opportunity to open a new position of clinic coordinator to manage these services themselves.

It is important to note the gendered nature of these coordinators who are providing clients with care. Dr. M. of the Brno clinic said, "Of course we have for each language a coordinator, all of them are female, and all of them speak fluently in the native language: Italian, French, English, and German. And you need to have a staff that speaks at least one foreign language, so maybe everybody speaks English and we have Italian-, French-, German-speaking doctors." Coordinators bridge the Czech host role as well as the medical side. Ludmilla was a newer coordinator, hired in 2010 to help Lenka at the clinic. She claimed she was "half nurse, half coordinator." Ludmilla had lived in Chicago for many years before returning home to the Czech Republic. She described her role and work, also using affective discourse:

> I am a nurse when the English patients are here. I take care of them from time they walk in the clinic. It's possible for this, since we have seven consultations in one day. I have only a short time for everybody. But I try as much to take care of them, what they want, explain to them what's going on. I am present at the consultation with the doctor, and I do take care of them after the transfer, when I need to explain the future medication and things they are supposed to do and not supposed to do.

As IVF brokers become nearly obsolete, women like Lenka and Ludmilla are now the main artery of this global care chain. As the clinics become savvy and create their own websites in various languages, they are able to cut out the middleman.

Cindy remembers Lenka accompanying her to an ultrasound appointment, when they had to sit in the waiting room for a little while: "Lenka sat down with us while we were waiting for the phone to charge and really gave us all this information about where to go, telling us little stories about her family and her two kids. She was making great small talk and great eye contact. And she was squatting down, she didn't sit. I'm thinking she was very lovely and very helpful, just like what everyone has always said." Again, virtual biosocial communities prepare patients for service they will receive, and patients carry these images throughout their clinical encounters.

The Brno clinic also hired two new coordinators between my two visits in 2010 and 2011. Olga originally worked for Petra's IVF Choices. An attractive blonde, she charmed the North Americans who first came to Brno. However, after she had her own baby, she wanted to reduce her working hours. Around that time, the clinic contacted her and asked if she would work directly for it rather than for Petra. She felt torn and did not want to hurt Petra, yet the stable schedule of the clinic seemed more appealing than being on call 24/7. When I asked Olga what she did as coordinator for the clinic, she answered, "I take care of them while they want to be our patient." There has been a perceptible drop in business at IVF Choices, as Dr. M. claims that more patients are using the Internet to find out about the clinic directly.

From the perspective of patients, I quickly learned of customer dissatisfaction with IVF Holiday. During my first summer of research, I had assumed that all the North American patients traveled through a broker. When I met Leah early on, I learned how patients could work directly with clinics. Zoe describes a similar discovery. During her preliminary research phase, Zoe had first e-mailed IVF Holiday with a lot of questions. But then she realized that many of her questions were medically related, and she felt they should be answered directly by the clinic. "Because of the fact that I have high blood pressure and I'm on medication, I have other medical issues that I wanted to ensure that the clinic would be aware of. I thought that it would be best if I contact the clinic directly, because of the fact that it is an option." Zoe felt reassured when the clinic hired its own coordinator: "The clinic having a coordinator made it so much easier. A coordinator will give you all hotels that have a medical rate, will ensure that they pick you up at the airport and such. It's sort of like the coordinator will bend over backward to ensure that you have the best possible experience. Lenka and Kamila were just phenomenal because they fit right into that expectation, and I never turned back once I started really reading the information they were providing."

Czech clinic coordinators are lauded for their quick responses and high levels of organization. Ben, from Seattle, admires the Zlín clinic's self-presentation: "I think the way they scheduled it is appropriate, an exactitude about it. You know, it's, 'Be here at this time. We're going to do this.' They try not to leave a lot of gaps in time, try to make it as efficient as possible. One of the things that they've really done is they present a really good product: that cleanliness, that staff being able to communicate in a number of different languages."

As the Zlín clinic increased its efficiency and service, it seemed as if Hana and Tom's response time lagged in comparison. This threatened their survival in a fiercely competitive fertility holiday market.

Kate, my fellow Floridian, had initially considered using the services of IVF Holiday just as Zoe had: "I did in the beginning, especially because we'd never traveled here before. The forum was a big part of us deciding not to do that. People just felt the clinic was providing more services, and there wasn't much of a need to use a service like that." Kate had tried e-mailing Hana and Tom: "In the beginning I think that was the route that we were headed. We thought we were going to use them. Actually it was the timeliness of response. The clinic responded immediately, and it was at least a week and a half later that IVF Holiday responded to our initial inquiry. So I just kind of assumed that they weren't having an active role anymore." Among the other criticisms I heard about IVF brokers was the complaint that their websites were dated. In fact, the IVF Holidays website has not changed since the first time I viewed it in 2009.

Many North Americans like Leah and Faith, who have made several trips to the Czech Republic, noted changes in the clinics. Indeed, based on pictures taken by reproductive travelers who have been to Zlín, one can glimpse the extensive renovations the clinic has made over the years. Patients notice the clinic looking "vaster" or "newer" than in the outdated pictures they had seen on blogs and websites. The Zlín clinic, which first resembled an old, Soviet-style hospital with a rickety elevator, began to resemble a modern, chic business furnished by IKEA. Looking at the clinic from the outside and then going inside was like traveling through time. As Zoe, from Barbados, described it:

> It did not look very modern on the outside. In fact, it looked very institutional. In going into the building, even though the outside looked very institutional, the inside looked—well, there were many renovations going on at the time that we were there. Let's see, the pharmacy had just opened. They were just working on the cafeteria on the lower floor. The stairs going up to the second floor they were just installing when we were there. By the time we finished, they had put the railings on. So upon entering the building, you were like, "Wow, these renovations." Then once you go up the stairs, you saw the old doors and you're like, "Oh wow, they're doing an awful lot. They have to renovate this building." But then to go into the office, it was like a different planet. I mean it was very modern looking. Because of that time of year, they had the windows open; butterflies were flying around. It was really surreal. And they had the television and that type of stuff, it was very fashion forward. It seemed that once you walked through the door, you walked into a completely different place. And then again when going up to the third floor, it was a pleasant surprise to buzz through and see how modern everything looked. Even with the equipment that they had, that was also top of the line.

In 2011, the clinic in Zlín was in the middle of constructing its own accommodations for patients. Lenka was confident that this in-house hotel would only boost their business with foreign clients:

> I would say that we will have more patients from abroad, because we didn't advertise until now, and we were not prepared because of our capacities. Of course there was not any coordinator like now, and English-speaking doctors. Now we have three English-speaking doctors, another fourth will come, so they will be able to take care of more clients. And there will be [a] hotel for our clients. I would say seventeen apartments, so they will be together. They would like to make, for example, a relaxation room with Jacuzzi and massage. So I think it will be more advantageous for them, so the clients can come alone or with their partners for

[a] shorter period of time, because they will be together. The whole thing will be really very nice, it will be very modern. It's under construction right now. There is not any clinic with such services, so I think we will have more and more clients.

The repeated use of the word "modern" connotes progress and forward thinking, as if Czech clinics entering the global market acquire a more sophisticated modernity. In fact, I interviewed Abby via Skype in 2012 while she was staying at these new accommodations. She and I laughed at the fact that prudish North Americans probably would not appreciate the mirrored bathrooms. There are still areas in which Czechs have not completely mastered an understanding of North American clients.

Medical Tourist Activism

The biosocial virtual communities of reproductive travelers have grown in size and number at the same time that IVF broker roles have shifted. The skills and knowledge shared by early patient pioneers ensured that this global care route had been "well beaten." During my second summer in the Czech Republic, Dr. M. told me he noticed more North Americans traveling to Brno without the aid of IVF Choices: "This year I can see the patients are coming more independently. So there must be the information on the Internet how to solve all the issues, accommodation, transfer for clinic, everything, because now they come on their own." As more and more North Americans travel to the Czech Republic, they essentially write "do-it-yourself" guides for future patients with detailed online blogs of their trips. Increasingly, women are urging others to forgo the use of brokers altogether. In fact, I witnessed some couples expressing regret that they had hired a broker after seeing others who had gone without.

As shown in chapter 2, women who learn about foreign treatment options and consider traveling abroad for reproductive care often participate in virtual biosocial communities. Linda, a blogger, described how women interested in reproductive travel came together on the RESOLVE website: "So I got on there, and that has been just an absolute life saver. There was a group of women that had come to Zlín at the beginning of this year. This other woman that had gone through several IVFs in the

U.S. before looking for international ones started saying, 'Hey, does anybody know any more about this?' So all these women came together, and we all started communicating about it. There was a core group that came in June and a few more in July." Active on the RESOLVE website, Linda and other women "campaigned" to have the site give them their own group for women interested in traveling abroad for treatment (Speier 2011a:596). Someone posted a "roll call abroad," and there were 1,076 responses to this single post:

> We petitioned RESOLVE and it took several months to get our own section, and it's called "Seeking Treatment Outside the U.S." We finally got our own section, so now there's a division between people who have been and got pregnant and want to chat about certain things. Then there's one for people who are thinking about going, and veterans, so that they can give information. Those ones are basically for Zlín and [Brno]. Then I think there's some for Madrid, Spain, and I think the person from South Africa was going to start posting on there . . . and there was another woman who went to India, and we're trying to get her to post stuff on there . . . so we have more choices people can make.

Linda's description about the process of getting their own blog within RESOLVE parallels that of an activist/self-help support group. The positive spin placed on offering women "choice" signals the consumer element of these fertility journeys. Linda excitedly told me of the activity: "We've got . . . another batch of people that are looking for September. I think the next one she goes to [Brno] in September. We've got a couple people that are coming to Zlín for sure in October, and there's about four or five other women who are looking . . . to figure out if they can do it. They're going through the same questions that we had." The petitions and high rate of information sharing evoke consumer advocacy of reproductive travel, but the metaphor of "batches" of people means that the website is manufacturing patient-travelers (Speier 2011a:596).

Linda and Michael opted to organize their trip to Zlín without the use of a broker and closely followed the advice of women who had already been to the Czech Republic. They wanted to save the money they would have paid an IVF broker. Linda made sure that she blogged throughout her trip:

So every night, after we've done something here, whether it's information for the clinic, whether it be the zoo, whether it be Vienna for a couple days, the bus system, or the train system, we write detailed directions on how to do each of these things, so that we can share it with the next person. Because so many people have been so nice to share it with us, I wanted to contribute. It may not be much, it may or may not help anybody, but even if it helps one person make the trip less stressful and more enjoyable and successful, I'm thrilled.

Linda presents how the "roll call abroad" happened by framing it as an advocacy group where women were encouraging one another to take advantage of reproductive travel by paving the way with their stories. She describes a process of helping out future reproductive travelers with further knowledge of how to navigate their travels to the Czech Republic. Patients who are arranging their travel without the help of IVF brokers are assuming even more responsibility for their health. Biosocial virtual communities arm future patients with "survivor kits" for reproductive travel.

Websites of support groups are inundated with advice for future reproductive travelers. Leah claims that the people on the chats prepare you for the clinic visit. Leah remembers her first visit, before major renovations had happened: "We had seen pictures from people who had posted and when we saw the building, we said, 'Ah, yeah, very nice building.' The proper clinic was clean, we kind of thought the comparison to home is that everything at home is so sterile, and people have gloves, and anything they do, sheets and things. And here you've got open windows, and nurses walking around with no [underwear] on, and it's just a different culture. If you've heard anything, you kind of know what to expect." The pictures provided on support group websites or on personal blogs frame patient expectations so that patients know what they will see when visiting the clinic in Zlín or Brno. Josefsson (2006) has noted how online self-help groups exchange information as well as experiences. Fertility support websites act similarly, essentially framing future reproductive traveler expectations and experiences. April said about the forums: "I think the forums help with the normal expectations, because then you kind of get a sense of the average experience." Similarly, Janice and Craig spoke of how they turned to testimonials to learn what to expect, especially since they had not been through a cycle of IVF in the States.

Czech clinics benefit tremendously from the "free advertising" provided on various fertility websites. Lenka says it is the blogs that really get the Zlín clinic's name out there: "I would say whatever you tell the client, they can believe you or maybe they will not believe you. But if somebody was here, that is it. On the board, they explain everything. One client sent me just a part from the chat where they wrote about me, and I was really excited about the details. For example, they call us with special names. For example, they call my husband Mr. Muscle, and they have special name for everybody, like nicknames." The blogs essentially frame the expectations of future "batches" of patients. When photos are taken in the transfer room and the doctor is photographed as if he is a famous monument, the touristic elements blur with medical protocols. Reproductive travel websites offer an abundance of information on the pharmaceuticals involved in IVF. Medical advice is offered along with guidelines for traveling to the Czech Republic. Patients urge one another to demand a certain kind of treatment.

Janice talks about how information gleaned from websites shaped her own protocol in the Czech Republic:

> Well, doing the research on the Internet you find a lot of people that had already done IVF in the past, so they would carry what they knew from their past experience to here. So, for example, I read and I jotted down a protocol that you should be on antibiotics three days before, and your last pill should be the day of retrieval. So then, of course, when I was here, I didn't even think about it. I just assumed that you would get antibiotics. I'm not sure if that is because I'm used to before surgery, you have at least three doses of something. But here, we just requested to have antibiotics prior. . . . They were very, very open to any kind of suggestion. And of course we would take any suggestion as well, because we don't know.

In Janice's case, these patient communities frame new patient expectations of treatment and demands for tests, medicines, or procedures. We also witness a different relationship between patients and doctors in Czech clinics, as patients enter the clinic armed with their own expected protocols based on what previous patients advise them. Patients encourage one another to demand particular tests or procedures, advocating for one another as patient-consumers. For example, Valerie wanted an unnecessary PGD on her embryos, since she was using donated eggs and sperm, which had already been heavily screened. The clinic acceded to her wishes. The entrepreneurial clinic that will agree to particular demands will continue to gain foreign business.

Faith started a website for reproductive travelers devoted to IVF in Zlín as a way for women to provide testimonials and information. Interestingly, Faith had used IVF Holiday, yet she still wanted to provide more support and information for people traveling to the Czech Republic. Her website represents another path along the global care route of reproductive travel. Faith recalls that the website grew out of control, and she needed to enlist the help of other women to run it. Although she created the website as a form of support and did not intend to subvert IVF Holiday's business, this happened nevertheless. When I talked with her in December 2011, the website had a total of 384 members; by the summer of 2013, this number had grown to 576.

The reproductive travel industry is an expanding "global assemblage" (Ong and Collier 2005) of care, technology, and health. Rose and Novas have used the term "biomedical self-shaping" (2005) to refer to patients taking an active and dynamic role in enhancing their biomedical literacy. Associated with neoliberal models of health care is an increasing level of self-management by patients. Participants on blogs and forums encourage, and even urge, women to make the "extra effort" of working with the clinics directly in order to save money. April and Larry, who traveled to Zlín in June 2011, were urged to not use IVF Holiday by the members of the forum started by Faith. April said she had considered working with IVF Holiday at first, but "the forum was a big part of us deciding not to do that. People just felt like the clinic was providing more services and there wasn't much of a need to use a service like that." Over the past few years, as Czech doctors have treated hundreds of North Americans, Czech clinics have come to understand foreign patient expectations.

The initiative patient tourists take in seeking IVF abroad continues as they undergo treatment in the Czech Republic. American patients, who have often been through a cycle before, are known by Czech clinics for their organization, their promptness, their demands for service, and their knowledge about the treatment protocols. Jana, a coordinator, said of North Americans: "The people who already went through it, they are calmer and they joke a bit as well, and just take it how it is. Mostly, they know what to do, they take care of themselves . . . they can be very independent." Eva, another clinic coordinator, said, "The American patients are well prepared, like they know what is going on." Dr. M. concurred, saying that Americans knew the medicines and the treatments because of their earlier experience in the States.

Czech clinics have successfully assumed the intimate labor previously performed by IVF brokers. Clinics now have a handle on what North American patients expect and want. They can now coordinate the cultural differences at the clinic and the technological medium of the treatments. The website of IVF Europe promises, "We employ multi-lingual coordinators that will arrange your entire treatment plan. We would be happy to assist you with your travel preparation and sightseeing and entertainment arrangements during your stay in the selected town." Funding extensive renovations and building of en suite accommodations is like the claw of capitalist venture that feeds this medical business growth. Yet North Americans, strangely, do not see the profit motives. The next chapter follows North Americans as they try to experience the "vacation" portion of their fertility holidays.

A global medical tourism market brings the stratification of reproduction into sharp relief, and the Czech Republic occupies a particular niche in this neoliberal market. Its liberal legislation has enabled the expansive growth of private fertility clinics all over the country. The intimate labor of IVF brokers coordinates the first North American encounters with Czech clinics. For couples seeking IVF using an egg donor, their choices as patient-consumers are limited as clinical regulations regarding donation strengthen. Furthermore, clinics have begun hiring their own coordinators, effectively taking on the intimate labor needed to serve North American patients. As patient activist consumers, North Americans confidently travel this well-beaten global care route to Czech clinics. The next chapter interrogates the extent to which North Americans do experience a holiday while undergoing IVF abroad.

4

Contradictions of Fertility Holidays

Ok, so my frame of mind has been to kind of take this as a vacation and not think about what we're doing, because I figured there's no reason to stress myself out. There's nothing I can do to influence the outcome. All I can do is have a good time, and make sure that we have a good time and have a good trip and hope for the best.

—Maureen

The IVF brokers brand "fertility holidays" as a package that promises the hope of a white baby, excellent care, and a vacation. However, scholars working in the field of reproductive travel have fiercely debated the proper label for those patients traveling abroad for care. Some have argued that the term "reproductive tourist" connotes pleasure and is therefore inappropriate (Pennings 2005; Inhorn and Birenbaum-Carmeli 2008). Others have argued that we should label these lower-class and lower-middle-class patients "reproductive exiles," since they are forced to seek treatment outside of their home countries (Matorras 2005; Inhorn and Patrizio 2009).

Do couples actually experience their travel as a "vacation" or "holiday"? Because IVF brokers lure North Americans with notions of a European vacation, and there are endless testimonials from couples who claim to have had an amazing trip, this issue merits closer scrutiny. The extent to which couples or women enjoyed a European vacation depended largely on their socioeconomic status. Only those who could easily spend $10,000 for the trip to the Czech Republic were able to afford additional weekend trips to Vienna or Budapest. For the majority, however, $10,000 was still expensive, and so they could only afford to travel locally. A small number of people were spending everything they had simply for the IVF, so they would mainly stay cooped up in the pension.

As we have seen, there are contradictions in patient reactions to infertility (working hard yet thinking positively), ARTs (which can be seen as both empowering and disempowering), and using the Internet (liberating in providing patients access to information, yet forcing them to be an informed consumer). The global terrain of reproductive travel only exacerbates the contradictions embedded in the movement of reproductive technologies across the globe (Ong and Collier 2005). It is precisely the term "fertility holiday" that embodies the ultimate contradictions of these North American experiences abroad. As Maureen and others embark on a fertility journey to the Czech Republic, they try to minimize the real stress of going through a medical procedure in a foreign place, and their narratives highlight the amazing vacation they had.

Many patients blog while they are abroad on their fertility holidays. However, they often write two separate threads, revealing the dual nature of these trips: one side is medical, and the other is about the vacation. Zoe said that she kept two blogs: "We had two blogs going. We had our vacation blog for a family member enjoying the Czech Republic and stuff like that. Then I had my infertility blog, which basically related to how I was feeling and what was going on." Patients describe adventuring through salt caves and trying new foods alongside their anxieties about egg removal and embryo transfers. Their blogs are filled with pictures taken with the doctor on the day of the transfer beside images of Prague Castle. Linda described the embryo transfer she had just undergone before meeting with me: "I felt the doctors and nurses were competent and they were even jovial and happy. So I took a picture with the doctor and the nurses before transfer, which I know would never happen [at home]."

The dual nature of fertility holidays can be seen in customer ratings of destination countries for IVF. Craig noted that one website rated countries in terms of fertility holidays, and that was what led him and Janice to choose the Czech Republic: "We hadn't put too much thought about the Czech Republic, but then we had started seeing reviews. Everything on the website where they had, based out of four stars rating, this is where they fall. Many other countries might have been two star, but this was actually rated as a four star. And that's the reason we leaned toward the Czech Republic in the end." Clinics are rated similarly to hotels or restaurants on travel websites like Yelp or Travelocity.

The experience of infertility is often referred to as a journey. Patients feel liberated by the possibility of reproductive travel. Linda, an older woman from Seattle, said her "journey would have ended" had she not found out about reproductive travel (Speier 2011a:592–593). The expression "fertility journeys" takes on additional meanings when patients embark on these global travel routes. Journeys can be literal, a trip to the Czech Republic; they can also be personal, a journey of discovery. I often heard couples say they were trying not to think about why they were in the Czech Republic. Taking a vacation is enveloped in a positive-thinking paradigm. The contradiction of medical holiday more broadly construed involves even further complications as women try to embody positive thinking by taking a holiday. However, it became clear that there were decisive breaks in the vacations couples experienced in the Czech Republic when the reality of infertility treatment and clinic visits interrupted their European vacation.

Although the price of IVF using egg donation is significantly less than in North America, it is still a hefty sum at $10,000. Thus, women suffer a lot of pressure to have a successful cycle. I witnessed many women internalizing lay medical admonitions that they must not be stressed when undergoing treatment. The terminology used by Californian Maureen, who claimed she was trying to be "Zen," evokes a New Age ideology of positive thinking that is pervasive in North America. It must be reiterated that many North Americans understand fertility holidays to be another step in their journey. When we were chatting after her transfer, Linda kept saying that she was simply thankful at having another start, another beginning in her attempt to get pregnant: "I'm thanking everybody, and they're like, don't thank us until you get pregnant. I'm like, no, you don't understand, I'm not thanking you if I have a child; I'm thanking you for the opportunity to have a child because this opportunity would not exist. So, yes, I'm really hoping. I'm trying to be positive hoping it all works. Will I be disappointed if it doesn't? Of course. But the fact that I have the opportunity." Again, we see a continuous thread in the way women speak about trying to be positive. Here, trying to be positive means considering your trip to be a vacation. If women successfully experience a vacation, they are properly relaxing, which is a strategy to increase their chances for success. This positive thinking essentially perpetuates the weighty personal responsibility women assume for their reproductive health.

A Space of Hope and Bonding

When I first traveled to Zlín in the summer of 2010, I followed Hana's advice to stay at the pension used by the majority of North Americans. Testimonials heap endless praise on the pension and paint the Czech hosts as kin rather than business owners. This bed-and-breakfast-like pension is run by a nuclear family. The ten-unit house sits atop a hill overlooking rolling fields. This small business, with its generous, warm service, is a central link in the global care chain of reproductive travel for North Americans in the Czech Republic.

I was unlucky the first summer I traveled to Zlín, since the month I stayed there was very quiet, and the often praised Mareka was out of town. I happened upon her sullen husband, Tony, who tended to work in the background or served as a chauffeur for guests. As I rode in the taxi to the pension that first summer, I became more excited with every turn the driver made up a steep hill. Colorful flowerbeds lined the boxy houses along the drive, and small dogs barked at us from well-kept yards. The pension's front door was locked, so I sneaked around to the side house where the owners lived to see if anyone was home. The taxi driver used his mobile to call the number posted on the door for me, and I was relieved that he did not leave me stranded on this lonely hilltop next to the quiet, three-story house. Thankfully, Tony soon arrived from his trip to the supermarket at the bottom of the hill. I was struck by his typical Czech brevity and wondered how his wife could possibly be the fount of warmth everyone had written about on blogs. By the end of my monthlong stay, Tony had warmed up a bit and whispered to me conspiratorially that I should book my stay with them directly the next summer. I had used my connection with Hana's IVF Holiday to arrange my first visit, and I foolishly realized that that connection may not have been the way to win Tony's heart. He wanted all of the profit next time.

Luckily, I was able to finally meet Mareka upon her return from her holiday a few weeks later. I always came upon Mareka while she was cleaning, speaking with a friend outside on a picnic bench, or serving cappuccinos. Mareka, in her midthirties, always seems to be breezily entering a room with positive energy. Mareka hugs people and serves breakfast with a huge smile on her face. Her work can also be considered "intimate labor" (Boris and Parreñas 2010). She has waited up for very late arrivals. This custom of greeting newcomers at all hours of the night evokes a sense of homecoming, even for those who were first-timers. Mareka's welcoming personality makes North Americans feel at home, since they feel drawn to her warm spirit and energy. In North American culture, the "intimate" is "connected to home, bourgeois domesticity." However, it is precisely those "social relations marked by intimacy" that are "central to the structures involved in the neoliberal processes of the global economy" (Cabezas 2011:5).

Because North Americans stay from ten days to three weeks, they often rent apartments so they can cook. Various couples claimed that the pension was the best part of their trip. Maria raved, "Oh, we love the pension, absolutely love it. It's exactly what you need. It's not extravagant. It's not a bunch of frills and whistles. We rented the apartment upstairs and you have everything you need. . . . I love the way that it's all very compact and organized . . . and it's not the consumer frame of mind over there." Again, Maria avoids noting the capitalist framework of the travel industry and finds comfort and care living amid the "simple" homelike apartments. The effusive affection felt for Mareka and her family reveals the way "patients tend to romanticize the level of care and the relationships with their practitioners despite the language and cultural divides" (Whittaker and Speier 2010:373). We must consider the pension, then, as a central point of destination, one that imparts the feeling of relaxation and comfort while abroad.

North Americans traveling along this hopeful route to creating a family become enmeshed in one another's lives while staying at the pension. As scholars of those who travel abroad for international adoption have described it, "Others who traveled and lived together when they collected their children often create a common history" (Howell 2006:77). In a similar vein, the pension becomes a place of origin for North American reproductive patients. Patients were well aware when a new couple was due to arrive at the Czech accommodations, since there was a running record of dates within virtual biosocial communities. Patients would notify me when a new couple was expected to arrive, and I noted the ease with which they all communicated immediately, given their shared point of origin for a family via ARTs in the Czech Republic. Even further, the pension acts as a haven for reproductive travelers. The intimate labor of Mareka and her family is a crucial link in the global care chain of North American reproductive travel in the sleepy town of Zlín. North Americans imagine their hosts as family members and speak highly of them, using charged affective discourse.

Sharing Meals, Sharing Stories

As a small town of 75,000, Zlín offers little to do. Mareka provides breakfast every day. As Mareka lets people know when other Americans will be arriving at the pension, she creates and sustains bonds for her guests over yogurt, granola, eggs, fresh bread, and cappuccinos. Breakfast is the social hour of the day. Couples make plans to visit the zoo, the local mall, or nearby castles. Conversations move easily from discussions about medication doses, transfer dates, or egg quality to more mundane travel topics like Czech food. While abroad, couples feel the weight of their secrecy lifted. They are aware that Czechs probably know why they are there, at least in the town of Zlín, which does not otherwise experience a lot of international tourism. They can openly speak about their infertility and its treatment around the breakfast table at the pension, as people compare their endometrial lining, numbers of embryos, and day of transfers, often going in to the clinic together (see figure 4.1 for an image of the recovery room).

Many couples find these shared meals comforting. Daniel felt like he and Maureen were part of a community: "And then to have all these other people here that are like, 'We had twins on the first try, now we're here again.' And then everyone else you know, 'We're going [to the clinic] on Monday, We're going on Tuesday.' We went out with a couple that just had their transfer and they were heading back home in a couple days, and it just makes you feel like you're a community, part of a system that works." According to Daniel, couples who meet one another learn things over breakfast and also see proof of the technological success of IVF embodied by the children of return guests. Pension owner Mareka is truly happy when she witnesses such community, and I frame these friendships as a form of social kinship (Speier 2015).

After their lengthy stays, couples often feel sentimental and sad when they are preparing to leave. Before their departure, they sign the pension's guest book. Patients promise to return, as family members are wont to do. People thank Mareka effusively for the care her family pro-

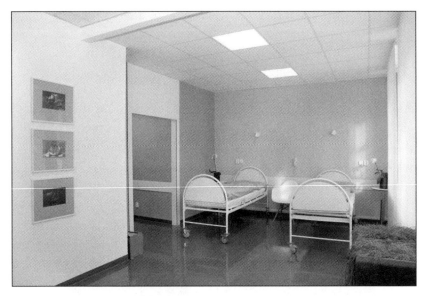

Figure 4.1 Recovery room of the clinic.

vided. I, too, experienced these close bonds with some of the patients, finding it hard to not shed a tear when saying good-bye to women I had spent several weeks getting to know.

Keep Coming Back!

The compulsion associated with reproductive technologies is refracted on a global scale when opportunities to travel for IVF open up to North Americans, feeding the desire to travel a new route to possible parenthood. Women feel obligated to try the newest reproductive technologies in their search for alternative ways to have a family. This compulsion is often framed in moral terms as a form of social control that pressures women at the same time that it empowers them. Rapid changes in the field of assisted reproduction may, in fact, confuse women and pull them in multiple directions.

Even though couples try to remain positive while in the Czech Republic, they also keep in mind how many more trips they can afford to take in case their cycle does not work. Even during their first stay (when I met them), both Maureen and Daniel wondered aloud how they would be able to return. Daniel knew it would take time to earn the money for future trips, which would cost them even more time, which in turn would inhibit the success rate of the cycle—a conundrum.

As shown throughout this book, individuals now assume responsibility for their health in a global neoliberal marketplace of options. In addition, positive thinking is a pervasive discourse that infertile women and couples use often. Chapter 1 outlined the ways women try to think positively while navigating the world of infertility. Positive thinking implies that what you think will manifest itself in the world. You change the world with your thoughts, exerting a force. When women experience infertility, they are often told that they will get pregnant if they simply relax. Despite the very real stress of infertility, the etiology of infertility is explained by the power of the mind. Infertile patients often blame themselves as they assume moral responsibility for their health care and succumb to the ideology of positive thinking. They think they may not be healthy enough, or that they have not been thinking positively. Because it is a woman's body that is the focus of reproductive technologies, women tend to blame themselves for an inability to get pregnant. They feel guilt, shame, and sadness, often claiming that they feel "broken." Dr. R. of the Zlín clinic claimed that 30 to 40 percent of infertility cases are caused by psychological issues. The problematic aspect of this view is that women often blame themselves and become caught in a vicious cycle of worry, stress, and trying to relax. Once they land upon the option to take an IVF vacation, this pressure to relax grows even stronger.

In my interviews with patients I met in the Czech Republic, I asked them what advice they would give to someone experiencing infertility. Many said they would say not to "give up." Claudia said, "If they really, really wanted to have a child, I'd say don't give up, because there is proof that you can be successful. We thought our options were closed and we thought it was so expensive here. I'd say don't give up if you really want to do it." This advice is what others had given them, and it is laden with American values of hard work and unending perseverance.

Even when couples have a successful cycle, and even when couples have twins, they still feel compelled to return to the Czech Republic. Jenny admitted she had told herself she would not return to the Czech Republic, yet she found herself coming back for a second round (and returning for a third time after I met her): "We were saying we would never come back if we were successful. And then they [their twin children] were just too cute." Some women would hide from their friends and family the fact that they were returning to the Czech Republic, to avoid possibly being judged as too voraciously hungry for a child. Couples tend to experience their infertility journeys vis-à-vis others' journeys, and there is surveillance among them. An unspoken expectation, even judgment, was that one child should suffice for infertile couples. Abby was well aware that her colleagues thought she should be happy that she had one daughter from IVF, and that couples should be happy with what they have and not overconsume: "When I tell my colleagues, they're like, 'Oh you're going again. Are you crazy?' 'Cause I was already lucky enough to get pregnant." Again, a successful cycle is correlated with gambling and luck. When I met Abby later, she admitted, "IVF is addictive." Couples are well aware of this contradiction: that common opinion holds that one child should suffice for an infertile couple, yet they feel compelled to return to the Czech Republic for more cycles.

Relax! The Ultimate Contradiction of Fertility Holidays

Women often hear from friends, doctors, and the media that they will get pregnant if they simply relax. It is as if wishful, positive thinking can beat the odds. The IVF brokers build on this assumption in promising a vacation. In addition, they offer couples who have been told they need to relax a potential way to do this. One testimonial claims, "I know being so relaxed and calm helped us get pregnant with twins on our first trip!" I argue that the most insidious contradiction of reproductive travel builds on this common idealistic etiology of infertility.

In branding "fertility holidays," brokers claim to offer patients both a more affordable and a less stressful IVF treatment. Petra, owner of IVF Choices, claimed that she tried to offer a "low-stress" alternative. Brokers want people to feel like they are tourists. They even link patient success rates to conceptualizing their trip as a vacation. Hence, social understandings of infertility become ethical constructions of who deserves to get pregnant. The woman who can treat the Czech trip as a vacation will signify to others that she is worthy of getting pregnant, that she can in fact relax.

Multiple patient testimonials on broker websites claim the couples had a real vacation while getting treatment. These testimonials perpetuate this key component of positive thinking, linking patients' "vacation" to their successful cycle in the Czech Republic. Deborah said to me over the phone, "If it didn't work, we got a wonderful vacation." Tracy kept saying to me as well, "For $11,000 we had a European vacation, made the best of friends, and came home with two babies. That is the best part." Maria also repeatedly said that it was a "worry-free" vacation and that the cycle was much less stressful than in the States. It is no wonder that Hana of IVF Holiday used Maria as a constant referral for people wanting more information about the trip.

The couples I met often spoke about conscientiously trying to treat the trip like a vacation, as though it was their job to consider it from a particular perspective. Daniel described this cyclical mental process:

> I've treated it like a vacation, as much as possible. I don't think about the clinic when I'm not there. I try not to anticipate. Maureen gets herself worked up sometimes, but you could hardly blame her. I have a tendency to get anxious if I dwell on it. I can spiral, where [I] don't enjoy the rest of my trip. So I've been purposefully throwing it all away. I went to Prague like we were just planning a vacation to Prague. That's how I treated Prague. We just did sights, we didn't really talk about the clinic. That's how I've been. Like even today, we look forward to getting massage, not thinking about getting an embryo transfer.

I witnessed patients trying to experience or understand their trip as a vacation. Yet this becomes contradictory when it is a directive. And, as with any vacation, there will be moments of stress (such as having difficulty finding one's train, or running to catch that train). The weather does not always cooperate. Kate said that there were times during their travels when they weren't thinking about their fertility treatment. When she had been in the United States, it had been "fertility, fertility, fertility," which affected how she (or any patient) went through a cycle emotionally.

Patients remember their cycles in North America as stressful. This stress was often compounded by the secrecy of infertility, which made it difficult for patients to leave work at a moment's notice to go to the clinic for multiple tests. Petra spoke of how stressful treatment is in the United States, because women typically maintain their work schedules when undergoing treatment. They find themselves juggling their busy lives with the clinic's demands for frequent and spontaneous tests. Julie, from South Carolina, admitted that it was stressful hiding her treatment by sneaking off to the clinic. Treatment in the Czech Republic, in contrast, is characterized as less stressful than in the United States.

Mareka noted a shift in the activities of North American patients over her years of hosting. She said that the first couples who stayed at her pension did not travel as extensively as they did in 2011. The IVF brokers might have increased their advertising of possible destinations for couples. And, as testimonials began to pour in affirming that couples had actually experienced a vacation, future couples increasingly began to seek that vacation element. They became fearless travelers in numbers, and the vacation element increasingly became a crucial selling point and element to assure couples of a successful cycle.

The extent to which patients traveled while in the Czech Republic varied not only by socioeconomic status but also by their level of comfort with European travel. However far they traveled, North Americans would venture on excursions to take their mind off the fact that they were going through treatment. Zoe said that she and her husband traveled to make it a "balanced experience." They wanted to go somewhere to get away from the clinic, if not mentally, then at least physically. It seems as though couples are engaged in mental acrobatics, seeking to avoid thinking about the reality of their medical situation and treatment, and diverting themselves with castles—though never quite fully.

Brokers told me that the couples who treat their trip as a vacation are the ones who have a successful treatment. Hana, of IVF Holidays, divided her clients into two main groups: the ones who go with the flow, and the ones who have to control everything. Embedded in this classification is an insidious denigration of the women undergoing IVF. More important, it indicates the ways that brokers encourage women to shoulder the responsibility for having fun. Taking a vacation is paradoxically hard work.

Vacation Interrupted: "Stirrups at the End"

Couples I met who were using IVF brokers did feel that the trip would have been too stressful without the brokers' services. As I sat in Julie's living room in South Carolina, her husband was busy in the background feeding and then bathing their three children. He rarely spoke, though he did joke that when they arrived at the Prague airport, they met this man who did not speak English and who handed them a cell phone with someone speaking English telling them to get into the car for a three-hour ride to their destination. The husband wryly noted that the guy could have killed them. This humorous memory indicates moments of panic or stress, when their vacation was interrupted by the reality of their visit.

While speaking to a doctor in Atlanta, I asked if he imagined IVF to be more relaxing for couples who travel abroad. He scoffed, "Silly. You're in a country that uses a Cyrillic alphabet and you don't know how to get on the damn bus. You know that's bull, that's just bull." Hana did admit that most couples find Czech culture "strange." While the Czech language does not in fact use a Cyrillic alphabet, the language is difficult for most patients to navigate. Alida and Allan, a couple from Texas, said that it had been "overwhelming" to travel around the Czech Republic. Thus, while patients try to embrace their trip as something relaxing, as with most travel, they also face stressful situations.

I characterize April and Larry as a couple who tried to act like tourists. They explored nearby Austria, Poland, and Slovakia after renting a car from the owners of the pension. They admitted that it would be nice not to have to see a doctor, to truly be on vacation. Larry had wondered before they left the United States if they really would be able to just get away, and indeed they had. But when they came back to Zlín for their egg retrieval, they had what they later described as a "reality check." The number of eggs retrieved during an IVF cycle may vary greatly (I heard of numbers that ranged from five to twenty-six), and women often compare their numbers over breakfast. April's egg retrieval produced only six, whereas her friend Jessica had announced eighteen. Given the stark difference, April felt disappointment and stress over her lowered chances for a successful cycle.

Over the course of the three to five days following egg retrievals, couples find out how many embryos developed in vitro. These days were often punctuated by feelings of joy or despair. Despite her plenitude of eggs, Jessica was disappointed when she had only three embryos, since most couples talk about freezing embryos for possible future visits (the language used is that of "banking" or "saving" for future trips). Couples inevitably felt sad if they did not have this option. It is during the time after the egg retrieval and before the egg transfer that stress impinges on couples' vacations.

Angela and Chris felt like teenagers backpacking through Europe, especially because they had not had two weeks of vacation in a long time. Chris said, "Zlín is an interlude to a really nice trip." In other words, Angela and Chris did not think of Zlín as part of the vacation, instead describing it in terms of a stopping point, the "stirrups" at the end of a European vacation (stirrups evoking a gynecological visit for North Americans) (Speier 2011b:20). Angela said that even with the process of an adoption happening at home in Chicago, she still felt a lot of pressure to conceive.

A petite Floridian, Kate had lots of nervous energy the morning before her transfer. She could barely eat her breakfast, and she was on the verge of tears as we took a walk outside to try to calm her nerves. Alison, who had already done a cycle in North America, tried to assure her that the transfer is an easy process. Kate admitted that she could "depress the hell out of" herself if she thought about her infertility for too long. Despite real attempts at experiencing a vacation, IVF reality broke through the vacation at crucial moments.

Dangerous Decisions

Who should have the power to make decisions in each of the
troubling situations where a choice has to be made about the
selection of an embryo?
—Nikolas Rose, *The Politics of Life Itself*

The fact that couples travel such a great distance to cut costs means they frame decisions about embryo transfers in terms of cost-effectiveness. The embryo transfer is an emotionally filled moment for couples that is definitely not part of the holiday experience. I witnessed couples snap at one another before their appointment. Tears were shed when couples saw their embryos. A critical moment comes when a couple has to decide how many embryos to transfer. I heard on multiple occasions that couples found themselves arguing in front of the embryologist as either the husband or the wife pushed for a higher number of embryos to transfer, to increase chances of conception. During the emotionally charged moment of the embryo transfer, couples must again make weighty decisions about the future of their embryos. Depending on the number of embryos that fertilized, they may opt to freeze a certain number and bank on a future trip back to the Czech Republic. I also heard endless comments of "two for the price of one," evoking hope for a twin pregnancy. However, there are potential dangers in transferring too many embryos. Pregnancy with multiples can lead to health complications for both the mother and the future children. Miscarriage may occur, and it is simply more physically taxing on the mother to carry multiples.

The following is one example of the contradictory nature of reproductive travel, whereby patients assume responsibility for stressful decisions as consumers. Faith told me how she had decided to transfer four embryos the first time she did a cycle in the Czech Republic. She explained how she made her decision:

> So, I had done a lot of research prior to either IVF cycle. I knew the dangers. I know the dangers of transferring too many. I know it's a gamble. I made an educated decision myself. This was not some crazy person. I was having to factor in all of our circumstances: the fact that this was our only trip, the fact that freezing one embryo and coming back for that one embryo is not cost-effective. If we had the money to come back and do another fresh cycle and freeze any from that, and then do another frozen cycle, I would have made that choice: to freeze one embryo. But I didn't want to just transfer two and freeze two, because I didn't want to lower the odds for this trip.

Faith put her body under pressure by transferring four embryos (more than the embryologist recommended). She weighed financial possibilities for future trips. She did a cost-benefit analysis of each option, with her body the stage for her contradictory experience. Like "professional guinea pigs," reproductive travelers who opt to put their bodies at more risk are following the "neoliberal imperative for individuals to feel they are making their own choices and for them to take responsibility for their own actions that may put them at risk" (Abadie 2010:160).

At the moment of embryo transfer, couples make choices based on what is cost-effective. This is problematic, since women put their bodies at risk when they transfer too many eggs. Recently, the Czech government has agreed to increase the number of cycles covered by insurance to four as long as the woman has only one embryo transfer per cycle. It is general knowledge that having multiples puts women and babies at greater risk and also costs medical systems money in cases of early birth.

Czech Clinic Touts Positive Thinking

Heeding expectations for individuals to assume responsibility for their health in a neoliberal model, North Americans again try to think positively. Patients self-monitor their attitudes as they go through treatment. Daniel and Maureen, together since college, talked of consciously trying to treat their trip "like a vacation . . . except when we were at the clinic." Daniel knew he could get anxious; Maureen could "spiral." She had nearly broken his heart when she labeled her body as "broken." During our interview, Daniel spoke in terms of his "hope" for a "karmic" world, where after a long time of trying, they would have a successful cycle. He said, "I believe in the power of positive thinking; you can make it happen."

A music instructor for an elementary school in Memphis, April had brought relaxing meditation music with her on her transfer day, trying to instill relaxation and positive thinking. Many couples, including Linda and Michael and Claudia and Ben, often talked about trying to be positive. Doug talked about how he was "thinking positive." Couples also spoke in terms of "fate," as when Maureen said, "If it is meant to be, it will happen." Jenny, the hardworking researcher, also said she would read a failure as a "sign." Yet, she still traveled back to the Czech Republic for a fourth attempt after her third ended in miscarriage, selectively ignoring the "signs."

On another level—and in addition to patients embracing the self-blame inherent in prescriptions to relax and think positively—those who are positive thinkers are deemed good people, or those who deserve to be parents. Individuals who are positive thinkers are worthy of getting pregnant. For example, Cindy referred to herself as a "positive person," indicating her moral worth to become a mother who would stay at home to raise her child. I witnessed moments of judgment if a couple perceived as "undeserving" had a successful IVF cycle and others did not. People try to rationalize and make sense of the success rates, or wrestle with their worldviews when their expectations do not pan out. For example, Claudia, who self-identified as "healthy" and a positive thinker, remembered a previous trip with another woman who was very negative about the whole thing but had *still* gotten pregnant. Claudia spoke of this as a cause for wonder.

The clinic has profitably embraced the ideologies of positive thinking and hard work that pervade the lives of American patients. Lenka, the clinic's main coordinator, told Daniel: "The only people who don't get pregnant are those who stop trying." Daniel found this statement to be empowering, whereas I considered it aggressive self-promotion and marketing. The risks of ovarian cancer, ectopic pregnancy, multiple births, and ovarian hyperstimulation, not to mention the psychological and emotional stress associated with in vitro fertilization, are inevitably downplayed in this assertion, which reveals another layer of contradiction that imbues "fertility holidays" of North Americans in the Czech Republic.

As we have seen, the social community that is built at the favorite pension offers a safe haven for North Americans doing IVF in the Czech Republic. They enjoy quality time with one another, and their biosocial communities shift from virtual worlds to actual friendships. As friendships are built abroad, patients enjoy the community they share with others who have similar problems.

Patients consciously attempt to consider and experience their journeys to the Czech Republic as "holidays." In so doing, they are perpetuating the everyday rhetoric that a relaxed woman is more likely to get pregnant. Despite the $10,000 price tag and the real stress and worry women experience, they claim to be experiencing a vacation, particularly when they have a successful cycle and write testimonials. This vacation element is a crucial yet contradictory component of "fertility holidays."

As patients are making weighty decisions at a Czech clinic, the vacation portion of their fertility holiday comes to an abrupt halt. The reality of their visit culminates at the embryo transfer, and women usually choose to stay in bed the following day, often eating pineapple, which is said to be good for the uterine lining. This chapter has shown the strength of social kinship bonds that develop among couples who suffer infertility as they undergo similar journeys together in the Czech Republic. Although they are strangers in a strange town, they bond instantly over newly shared genealogies. They continue to monitor their attitudes and frames of mind, heeding the advice of brokers and clinicians to relax and enjoy their European vacation. They believe that if they relax, they will increase the likelihood of getting pregnant. The clinic plays a hand in encouraging this self-management by patients. I argue that fertility holidays are fraught with intense contradictions, particularly in this notion that couples must embrace the notion they are on vacation.

The next chapter follows North Americans as they return home and shows the ways in which the social kinship bonds formed at the pension and clinics abroad are sustained. As infertility routes diverge, couples still participate within these (once again) virtual communities of social kinship. In addition, they continue to return to the Czech Republic, whether they are successful or unsuccessful, showing the heady effectiveness of intimate labor provided by the Czech clinics.

5

Separate but Connected Paths

It will be crucial for further policy ethnography and analysis
in this area to address the ways family planning takes place
as the sharing of reproductive dilemmas, and how this involves exchanges of information over time between kin, not
only prior to, but long after the birth event.
—Monica Konrad, *Narrating the New Predictive Genetics*

It was spring 2012, and I was sitting in my backyard in St. Petersburg,
Florida, drinking a cup of coffee and feeling excited anticipation. I would
be moving to Texas for a new academic position later that summer, but
before I moved I would embark on a monthlong road trip across the
United States to follow up with couples I had met in the Czech Republic
over the past several years.

Luckily, Leah from Toronto had a vacation home in Fort Myers
Beach, Florida, and I was able to make the two-hour drive from St. Petersburg to catch up with her. I was also able to meet her husband, who
had not been in Zlín when I had met her, as well as their eleven-year-old
son and the twins, successful "souvenirs" from her last IVF cycle in the
Czech Republic. Leah had a knack for articulating the big picture, and I
appreciated her candor in speaking of the difficulties of raising twin tod-
dlers. She admitted that their beach getaways to Florida would no longer
be restful. She was thankful, of course, knowing that she was one of the
30 percent success stories to emerge from Moravia's ARTs. This chapter
traces the varied routes North American couples continued along upon
returning home from their fertility holidays in the Czech Republic.

Those I met over the course of my research know reproductive travel
to the Czech Republic is simply one route among many in their "quests"
for parenthood (Janzen 1982; Inhorn 1994). Leah referred to the various
paths as resembling a flowchart that could include adoption, foster parenting, or resignation to having a childless marriage. Leah claimed that

a couple who opts to go to the Czech Republic to use IVF with an egg donor must be open to the idea of having a nongenetic child:

> And if you want a family, there is a way to do it. It's what are you open to doing. But when someone isn't interested in adoption or isn't interested in considering genetics other than his own, OK. Well here's your set of options. You almost want to make a flowchart of this, this, and this and go this route. Nothing says you can't go more than one route at once. If you want a family, there's a way to build it. You have to be open to whatever that might be until your flowchart comes to an end.

I traveled across North America following up with couples I had met, as I had with Leah and her family. I was able to meet some for the first time in person if we had Skyped previously. Some of the reunions were disorienting at first, since we were meeting in very different spaces than the Czech clinic or pension. It was often a heartwarming get-together, and I shared many meals once again with couples in California, Florida, Wisconsin, Nebraska, Washington, and Quebec. I was able to follow up with most couples, though I was unable to locate some. I assumed they were possibly grieving another failed cycle, or they wanted to forget that they had traveled abroad to start a family.

Table 5.1 Children Conceived via Fertility Holidays

Couple	Home	No. of Trips	No. of Children from Czech Republic	No. of Other Children
Tom and Hana	Ohio	1	Twin girls	
Juan and Anita	Indiana	2	0*	
Lauren and John	Texas	1	0	3 (foster then adopted)
Janice and Craig	Florida	2	1 boy (1st cycle)	
Leah	Canada	3	Twins, boy and girl (3rd cycle)	
Valerie and Dan	California	1	0	1 boy (adopted)
Maria and Ryan	Oklahoma	3	1 boy (1st cycle); 1 girl (3rd cycle)	

Table 5.1 (*cont.*)

Couple	Home	No. of Trips	No. of Children from Czech Republic	No. of Other Children
Linda and Michael	Washington	1	Twins, boy and girl	
Faith and Matt	Georgia	2	1 girl (1st cycle); twin boys (2nd cycle)	
Petra	Georgia	11	1 girl (via surrogate); 1 girl	
Suzanne	Montreal	2	1 girl (1st cycle); 1 girl (2nd cycle)	
Zoe	Barbados	1	0	1 ("naturally")
Megan	Texas	1	Triplets	
Julie	South Carolina	1	Twins, boy and girl (1st cycle)	1 boy ("naturally")
Tracy	California	2	1 girl	
David and Kim	Washington	3	1 boy (3rd cycle)	
Angela and Chris	Illinois	1	0*	
Abby	Wisconsin	4	1 girl; 1 girl	
Kate and Charlie	Florida	1	0	
Alison and Andy	Minnesota	1	0	Twins(U.S. IVF)
Deborah and Mike	Louisiana	1	0	
Jessica and Doug	Nebraska	1	Twin boys	1 boy ("naturally")
Maureen and Daniel	California	3	0	1 girl (U.S. IVF)
Jenny and Elliot	California	3	Twin girls (1st cycle); 1 boy (3rd cycle)	
April and Larry	Tennessee	1	0	1 girl (U.S. IVF)
Cindy and Scott	Montana	2	Twin boys (2nd cycle)	
Alida and Allan	Texas	3	1 girl	
Joan	Northeast	1	1 boy	
Kay	Germany	3	0	

* Denotes no data.

Of course, the couples I met during the course of my research were on different points along their "quests" for parenthood. Table 5.1 presents the resulting children and the different points of my interlocutors' journeys. Some journeys of infertility ended successfully after the first trip to the Czech Republic; others entailed several more cycles of IVF abroad or at home. These couples are all along different points of the "flowchart" toward building their families.

Scholars have considered the ways that those who are using ARTs in their building of a family "are not discarding old cultural ideas about kinship but, on the contrary, are making every effort to preserve the notions of 'real' biological parenthood. Towards this end, they are reinterpreting the NRTs and their tricky implications so as to reconcile them with these core cultural notions of biological parenthood and the resulting family ideal" (Levine 2008, cited in Stone 2014:283). In the case of North Americans traveling to the Czech Republic for assisted reproduction, there is a heteronormative underpinning to these families bolstered by Czech legislation that denies treatment to single individuals or homosexual couples.

Heterosexual couples who are raising babies born of IVF using an egg donor in the Czech Republic employ two competing discourses: one that naturalizes the bonds between parent and child by using "resemblance talk," and another that argues for the continued importance of the hard work the parents employ while gestating and raising their children. "Women using donor sperm and/or donor eggs may focus on their pregnancies and birth processes as a way of assimilating their experiences into the 'normal' means of having a baby" (Cahn 2013:33). Strathern (2005) labels the new forms of families "recombinant" to speak to the way that different components of motherhood and fatherhood are being taken apart and put back together in new ways, in both conception and rearing procedures.

The hard work that North Americans assume upon their initial diagnosis of infertility continues to be a strong ethic when speaking of parenthood. Not one couple chose to live a childless life. Rather, most continue to work hard by seeking out other alternatives. "So strong is the normative mandate for reproduction, and individuals' desires to conform to these social expectations, that for some it is better to have a child that is conceived by the use of donor egg or donor sperm, and to keep the stigmatized conception a closely guarded secret, than to remain childless" (Gürtin 2012:96). I argue that return reproductive tourism reflects North Americans' notions of individualism as well as their hard work ethic, tied to the compulsiveness of reproductive technologies.

Despite the varied routes traveled by interlocutors, the majority become return reproductive travelers to the Czech Republic. This fact underlines the successful marketing strategies of Czech clinics and hosts who have assumed the intimate labor directed at North Americans (Boris and Parreñas 2010). It speaks to the central importance of care embedded within reproductive treatment. Patients' relationships with doctors, nurses, and hosts in the Czech Republic continue to grow, and patients feel like they are "coming home" whenever they return. Return reproductive tourism to the Czech Republic reveals the important dimension of care, with its expanded meanings for lower-class North Americans trying to create a family using ARTs.

Furthermore, the majority of the couples I met maintained the virtual communities they had built online and in the Czech Republic. I argue that the communal bonds that are developed online and in the Czech Republic continue when patients return home. As couples disperse to their scattered homes all over North America, the social kinship networks that they built continue to be central elements of their lives. These communities, based on a particular kind of family, are important social entities for couples. As we have seen, these communities are highly gendered. In her classic article, di Leonardo has written about the gendered nature of kinship work, which involves the "conception, maintenance, and ritual celebration of cross-household kin ties, including visits, letters, telephone calls, presents and cards to kin; the organization of holiday gatherings; the creation and maintenance of quasi-kin relations; decisions to neglect or to intensify particular ties; then mental reflection about all these activities" (1987:442). For those new mothers who are sometimes isolated when they stay home and raise their children, social kinship networks continue to be important sources of information and support. Given their common narratives of family origin, they continue to maintain these quasi-kin relationships with one another, largely online. This chapter considers the nature of this community of reproductive travelers, revealing the importance of intimate labor in sustaining families built using reproductive technologies abroad. Despite the different paths taken by the couples, these social kinship bonds remain.

The Best Souvenir

While patient-travelers are in the Czech Republic, many joke about their hope for the best souvenir: a baby. This motif of baby as a souvenir plays on the consumer element of reproductive travel. Susan Frohlick (2015) has also used the expression "souvenir babies" when speaking of European–North American reproductive mobility to Costa Rica. When female sex tourists have children with local men, Frohlick underscores the resulting commodification of kinship relations created and sustained within the tourism industry. Similarly, in the case of reproductive tourism in the Czech Republic, babies are also referred to as products. One blog post of a woman who was expecting read: "I came home with my own special Czech souvenir." April, from Tennessee, said, "I feel like we got a lot out of this trip, and hopefully we can bring back a souvenir or two." In fact, there is "an overall twin delivery rate of 25.7% and triplet rate of 2.5% following conventional IVF and ICSI cycles" (Gürtin 2012:105). On the day of their departure, Mareka at the pension presents her guests with bibs that say "Made in Zlín," one blue and one pink (see figure 5.1), which underscores the "buy one get one free deal" discourse of IVF (Gürtin 2012:106), as well as the heteronormativity of families created by ARTs in the Czech Republic. These bibs come in handy for those couples who do have twins, but not for those who are unsuccessful. Often, couples find themselves wondering what to do with such gifts when they do not get pregnant.

Janice and Craig, the two nurses from Florida, were "lucky"—they were one of the couples whose first IVF cycle in the Czech Republic was successful. I met them in Florida late in the spring of 2012, happy to catch them before I moved to Texas. We sat on the front patio of a casual Irish bar, where their toddler roamed about freely, since it was three o'clock in the afternoon on a Wednesday. Janice's hair was quite a bit shorter than when I had met her earlier, and Craig's was slightly grayer. They admitted that they were very nervous parents, given the high investment they had put into having their son.

Figure 5.1 Bibs given to guests from the pension owners.

Even "luckier" are those couples who have twins. Jessica and Doug had transferred three embryos, although the thought of triplets scared her. Nevertheless, they were the lucky ones who ended up getting "two for the price of one." I visited them in Nebraska in the summer of 2012, and we enjoyed a lovely meal of pork chops in their comfortable home. It was a beautiful summer evening, so Jessica and I decided to sit outside as the twins slept. As he had in the Czech Republic, Doug disappeared quickly after the meal. As I caught up with Jessica, I had another brief glimpse of how difficult it is keeping an eye on twins. Jessica told me that she would simply have to let one cry as she nursed the other one. She did admit: "We were pretty pumped when we realized we were having twins. Triplets really freaked me out. But yeah, the multiples thing . . . well, now that we have twins, the thought of having another set is a little bit intimidating. They're a lot of work." Aside from a funny birthing story of being surprised to find out they had two sons rather than the anticipated girl and boy, the two were very happy and aware they were "lucky." Again, the rhetoric of gambling and luck pervades conversations about successful IVF outcomes.

However, just as the discourse of luck existed alongside the discourse of hard work in attempts to get pregnant, when discussing the reality of raising multiples, the two discourses continued to pervade conversations. Raising multiples is a difficult grind for most parents. Francis Price shows how parents rarely envision the actualities of raising multiples, including the sheer physical exhaustion and the high financial costs, when undergoing fertility treatments. The fact that they want so eagerly to have a child influences their ability to envisage the reality of raising multiples, and there is a lack of information on the part of clinics: "The quest for a child becomes a quest for pregnancy, and is deemed a medical matter, thereby narrowing the time-scale and focus of concern, to the neglect of possible consequences in the long term" (Price 1999:59). There is a high rate of premature births (61.3 percent for twins, compared with only 13.5 percent for singletons) that increases risks to pregnant women and offspring and requires heavier monitoring by the health care system (Gürtin 2012:105). Not only may a woman's pregnancy be endangered by the presence of multiples, but the juggling that parents must manage once their offspring are born is difficult, particularly when the children are very young. When I interviewed Jenny after watching her twin girls during her embryo transfer, she admitted to me that she has no time for hobbies. "I pretty much spend the whole day . . . it's like treading water, or bailing water out of a boat with a hole in it. That's my day."

I witnessed this Sisyphean existence while following up with those couples who had had multiples. While we caught up in her air-conditioned Florida condo, Leah was very frank with me about how exhausting having twins is: "I don't think that multiple births are ideal on any level," to which her husband chimed in, "I wouldn't wish them on anybody." Of course they loved and cherished their children, but caring for them is enormously difficult. Just the summer before, I had been struck when even Hana the IVF broker had said she did not wish twins on anyone, given that her business led to the birth of many.

The gender of twins may also raise unanticipated costs or obstacles. Linda and Michael had one girl and one boy, which put them in an unexpected predicament of having to add onto their house when their children were older. Linda recalls when they first found out that they were having twins:

> Oh my gosh. We're having twins. Then we had to wait from that six weeks all the way to eighteen weeks. I had them check the sexes four times just to double or triple or quadruple check. We went to check, and they're like, "Baby A is a girl," and we're like, "Yay!" And they're like, "Baby B is a boy! You've got one of each, that's great!" I'm like, "What are we going to do? One bedroom, it's one bedroom." Everybody said the same thing, "Oh you got a boy and a girl, that's perfect," and I'm like, "They were supposed to be the same sex." We didn't get that relief, you know, and so it was kind of anxious until now. I mean . . . We'll make it work.

I could understand her worry as I noted the cramped living room, full of toys not only for the twins but also for her nephew, whom she also took care of during the day.

One of the pioneers of fertility travel, Faith, had been successful in having a baby girl as the result of her first Czech IVF cycle. She and her husband returned to the Czech Republic for a second try in the fall of 2010. As we caught up in December 2011, I watched the twin boys (resulting from her second trip) get into as much trouble as possible as we chatted for several hours. Faith admitted she is fortunate to have her younger sister living with them as an extra pair of hands. Her husband still worked three jobs and thus was often away from home. Faith is still an avid user of social media, to which I will return later, and her daily posts on Facebook are usually about the difficulties of motherhood, of raising three young children. As I was revising this chapter, Faith posted, "Twin moms, please tell me it gets easier!" Infertile couples who successfully have twins face daily challenges in raising multiples. The joke of "two for the price of one" is no longer repeated in the homes of Jessica, Linda, or Faith. What does get repeated, however, is how the children resemble one or both parents.

Discourses of Resemblance

Scholars of international adoption and ARTs have written about "resemblance talk" (Jacobson 2009). Heather Jacobson provides accounts of families who pursue international adoption, and the differences between families who adopt children from Russia and China. She describes the "interracial surveillance" that families with Chinese-born adoptees experience on a daily basis, while those families with children born in Russia can more easily evade such public surveillance and enjoy a sense of "biological privilege" (Jacobson 2009). As in the case of the families studied by Jacobson, those couples who opt to travel to the Czech Republic for IVF using an egg donor are also thinking about race and are choosing a route that will afford them "biological privilege." As discussed earlier, fertility holidays promise North Americans a "white" baby. Because couples traveling to the Czech Republic are also primarily white, they are hoping for shared ethnicity with their children. Bergmann, in his ethnographic research at Czech clinics, noted that German patients were also motivated by a desire to resemble the donor (2012:332).

Because many couples who use an egg donor hide this fact, they are hoping to model their family after nature, "passing for kinship" (Bergmann 2012:351). Secrecy is a strategy to "manage the genetic identity of their children" (Haines, cited in Nahman 2013:84). As I traveled across North America to visit couples who were raising their "souvenirs," I was struck by their usage of resemblance discourse. When I reunited with Maria and Ryan in Tulsa in the summer of 2012, we sat at a public park where her teenage sons could roam around freely yet also keep a protective eye on their two younger siblings, born via IVF. The Czech clinic had mixed Ryan's sperm with donated sperm, which Maria told me increased the odds for conception. However, immediately after, Maria pointed to her younger daughter and son and said: "I don't think we've really talked about that, but when they choose sperm donors, they choose quality of sperm, not necessarily characteristics of the person. I think it's kind of obvious where these came from. If that one [indicating to her son] were any more obvious, he would be a clone." In using the word "clone," Maria is speaking of what Sarah Franklin labels a "new conception model in which biology and engineering are united" (2012:39). She is naturalizing the technology that bound her child's connection to Ryan, and adamantly dismissing the possibility that he was conceived by donated sperm. The use of the word "clone" indicates a confluence of technology with Ryan's "natural" fatherhood. By calling her son a clone, Maria is underscoring the resemblance between her son and husband. Often, North Americans discuss likeness and resemblance of their babies who have been born, naturalizing their affective ties with their children conceived using donation.

In his now classic ethnography on an emerging biotechnology industry, Paul Rabinow wrote, "Biotechnology's hallmark, it could be said, lies in its potential to get away from nature, to construct artificial conditions in which specific variables can be known in such a way that they can be manipulated. This knowledge then forms the basis for remaking nature according to our own norms" (1996:20). The industry he writes of is intimately related to reproductive technologies, as couples are seeking technologies that will let them mimic a "natural" family. Sarah Franklin writes of the ways that IVF has introduced a new reproductive model, whereby the "'natural facts' of sexual reproduction are understood as engineerable, replaceable, and intervenable" (2012:37). In a similar vein, Roberts states, "The 'biological' had recently changed from fixed to malleable" (2008:81). Although most couples traveling to the Czech Republic are seeking an egg donor, they are seeking a donor who will ensure the most natural family, one in which the child resembles the parent.

In North American idealized notions of the family, Hertz claims, "genetic and social parenthood are supposed to overlap" (2006:55). Scholars detail the ways in which women who use ARTs must "reconcile the route they took to pregnancy with myth and folklore about the role of genetics in child development" (Hertz 2006:xvii). Nahman analyzes how "the process of becoming an ova recipient involves decisions about whether one would accept ova from another woman, and the strategies of negotiating the importance of genetics, the relevance of gestation of the ova and how aspects of a kind of biological thinking come in and out of recipients' ideas about having a child through donation" (2013:86). We can consider genetics as a "way of thinking about ourselves, our bodies, our families, our lives" (Rothman 2006:20), encouraging a distinction between the science of genes and the ideology of genes. In fact, we can also understand the "Standard North American Family," or SNAF, to be an "ideological code" (Smith 1993). Rothman writes that while scientists know genes are "one factor in a multifactorial process" (2005:60), the public understands "genes as determinative, genes as fate" (61). Genetics and Euro-American kinship are "conceptualized as originating through a substance," whereby "resemblance" is a discourse employed when speaking of how a family should look (Bergmann 2012:355). Rose similarly argues that "it would be foolish to deny the hold that this idea of genes as the 'blueprint of life' coding for our human-ness, intertwined with older ideas of heredity and the gene as the unit of inheritance, has had on popular imagination" (2007:45).

Alongside resemblance talk, couples often remarked on the beauty of their children. A common statement in the Czech Republic is that Czech women are the most beautiful women in the world. While I could accept the veracity of this statement looking around fertility clinics, it is obvious that Czech clinics are marketing not only white egg donors but also donors who adhere to particular Eurocentric notions of beauty. Offhandedly, I heard women refer to the beauty of their children and equate it with Czech beauty. When I was interviewing Abby, I commented that her daughter is gorgeous, and she replied, "They must have some good donors here." Beauty equates with being a "good" donor.

Jenny said that she and her husband, Elliot, had worried that Czech donors might be substandard, but she motioned toward her twins, saying that their nineteen-year-old donor "must have been pretty good-looking." The notion of a donor being "substandard" is complex and demands unpacking. It could be that the geographic region of Central Europe and its former socialist past lent Czech donors this substandard genetic identity. Implicit, also, is the notion that North American egg donors are the standard by which Jenny is measuring other nationalities. If price difference indicates different standards, then the fact that North American women receive eight times what Czech women do can reaffirm these notions. A global market economy and its differential price points of gametes then would be the indicator of whose genetics are standard and whose are substandard.

One reason a woman may opt to undergo IVF using an egg donor is her desire to experience pregnancy. In addition to proclamations of resemblance, North American women stress the fact that they are the ones who carry the baby to term, emphasizing the mother's gestational role. In so doing, these women are emphasizing once again their hard work as parents. They often attributed resemblance and rights as the social parent to the fact that the woman experienced the nine-month pregnancy, during which something, some sort of substance, must have been transferred to the baby in utero. Once the IVF is successful, women enjoy carrying and nurturing their baby. The woman not only gets to gestate the baby but also has a lot more control, something she has had very little of since the diagnosis of infertility. Linda, of Seattle, articulated why her pregnancy was so important to her: "I got to control the food that they got. That was the one thing . . . when you have infertility, there's so much you can't control. Here I am, I'm pregnant and I can control exactly what goes into making them. It was like for once I can control and I was very good. I ate healthy. I ate well. I ate whatever the doctor told me to eat. I had the most healthy diet—in huge quantities of everything. I ate fruits and vegetables, and all that meat that they tell you." The fact that Linda was "very good" again reflects the self-monitoring a woman assumes throughout the time she tries to get pregnant until the baby's birth, again assuming an individual moral responsibility for her health and the health of her child. Linda chose to emphasize the pregnancy and the nourishment provided by the woman carrying the fetus. Her husband, Michael, also prioritized pregnancy in forming a bond: "I think there's more of a connection with your children. You give birth to them, not that there isn't a strong bond developed either way. But going through pregnancy with babies and giving birth is a whole process. I just think that it makes for a stronger bond." Linda and Michael are highlighting her role as the one who gestates their twins, a different tactic than couples who use surrogates along their routes to parenthood. Pande (2015) writes of surrogates in India forging kin ties with the babies they gestate, despite clinical attempts to urge the women to think of themselves as only a vessel.

During the summer of 2012, after a monthlong road trip zigzagging across North America, from Florida to Seattle, I first heard about epigenetics as I was catching up with Linda. She offhandedly described this new field:

I read a few real cursory studies with epigenetics, in that the mom, the person that gives birth, actually does contribute. I had never really thought about it before, but our kids . . . I mean we give . . . my mom and I joke about it. Our kids look like us, they have a lot of the same mannerisms. My mom's hair color is Ella's if she doesn't dye it blonde. I'm the only natural blonde. That's my mom's hair color, and she had those highlights as a little girl. It is just uncanny. We are certain, because a lot of our family was in Canada and the U.S. was in World War I and in World War II. We're thinking somebody was messing around over in that general area, because there are some definite traits. I mean you could find anything, but it's uncanny. So I don't know—epigenetics, luck of the draw, Lenka was a great coordinator, she did her best. I don't know.

Nikolas Rose also writes about this new field of epigenetics, "understood not merely as the mechanisms regulating gene expression that produce phenotypic effects from gene activity during differentiation and development, but also as heritable characteristics, some acquired over the life of an organism, that are not part of nuclear DNA sequences" (2007:47). Here we witness several strands of discourse employed by Linda to attempt to explain the resemblance she sees between her children and other family members. Either the resemblance is historically geographic or Linda as the one who gestated the twins contributed substances to the fetuses. It is revealing that she does not speak of her role as socializer of her children, yet she ends with a testimonial reaffirming the clinic coordinator's "matching" skills. Parents raising children born of IVF using an egg donor in the Czech Republic are naturalizing their bonds in various ways. Epigenetics complicates the reductionism of genetic thinking (Rose 2007:47). Just as Linda and other women may emphasize their role in giving birth, they will emphasize the "work" they have assumed throughout their journeys, in making endless trips to the Czech Republic and possibly going through difficult pregnancies that often required bed rest.

The Sticky Issue of Disclosure

Rothman has written about the ways in which rights discourse "makes so much sense in America" (2005:35). It seems also to be a European trend, where many nations are adopting laws that enforce open, non-anonymous gamete donation in the world of reproductive medicine (Knecht, Klotz, and Beck 2012). This move is linked to contemporary European "genealogical" ethics debates that have centered on the rights of a child and the child's "right to know" his or her genealogy (Konrad

2005:4). The dominant framework for these debates and discussions is mostly "modeled on the primacy of individual rights" (Konrad 2005:88).

European trends reflect the assumption that children born of IVF using donor egg will demand access to their biological origins. In fact, some scholars have documented children born via donation conducting Internet-based searches for half siblings and/or their donors (Klotz 2012:116). In fact, Klotz argues that it is practically impossible for medical institutions to keep kinship information away from families by donation (129), although that is what Czech clinics do assure clients and donors.

However, a recent study in Sweden revealed that only a very small percentage of children born via donation sought contact with biological genetic parents. Dr. O. in Barcelona said that Sweden had been the first country to do away with anonymity. He continued, "Only 3 percent of the babies born from the sperm donation request to learn the identity of the donors. It's more something that the parents claim, but it's not a real necessity in the babies, especially in donation." In thinking about this, however, I realize Dr. O. was speaking of sperm donation, which has different meanings in the public mind. Almeling (2007) has shown in her research that there are different valuations of eggs and sperm when it comes to the marketplace. Egg donation is given more weight, partly because of gendered notions of parenting in which traditional notions of femininity align women with the private sphere of the family and men with the public sphere. Given the weightier notions of motherhood, I assume more than 3 percent of the children born of IVF using an egg donor will want to know about their biological origins. Despite European trends, Czech doctors believe their piece of the reproductive travel industry pie depends on the anonymity of donation.

Parents of children born of IVF in the Czech Republic using anonymous egg donation must also wrestle with the thorny issue of disclosure. I was stunned to meet so many couples who had not discussed the issue of disclosure with one another before undergoing IVF using an egg donor. In part, this may be related to the compulsive nature of reproductive technologies. As Price (1999) has written about the inability of infertile couples to imagine the daily realities of raising multiples, these parents also do not think about if, when, or how they will disclose to their future progeny the nature of their birth stories. There are several issues at play when couples grapple with the issue of disclosure. They want to ensure the psychological health of their child, maintain the validity of their rights to parenthood, and ensure the social acceptance of their child. Intending to present their families as "normal," "parents wish to protect children and family from being stigmatized" (Snowden, Mitchell, and Snowden cited in Nahman 2013:84).

As I was speaking with Dr. R., the owner of the Zlín clinic, the topic of disclosure arose. In his years of treating both European and North American patients, he had discerned a notable difference between the two groups in attitudes about disclosure: "Most Europeans don't want to tell. You are their child. I don't know why, but Americans, if we are talking generally. . . . I think it will be better [if] I plan to say to my children. I don't know if it is good way or not. I think it's direct way to psychiatric [sic]. America it's very modern. Everybody has his own psychiatric work. Not in Europe, but in America there are a lot of very rich psychoanalysts."

It was apparent to me while conducting this research that there was great variability in terms of how North Americans thought about disclosure. However, the general trend of being "open" is connected to current notions about healthy parenting as well as discourse used in adoption circles. However, implicit in Dr. R.'s comparison is the idea that telling a child he or she was conceived using an egg donor will lead to psychological issues. I did meet reproductive travelers who were of the same mind, such as Valerie of San Diego, who said she did not want her child to know about her donation, since she assumed he might "freak out."

The issue of disclosure is inevitably tied to the issue of stigma. Infertile women who have experienced firsthand the stigma of infertility are sensitive to the possible stigma their offspring may face in being born from an egg donor. For example, Juan and Anita did not share with their families the fact that they were doing IVF with an egg donor; they did not want their child to be hurt. Anita worried, "The reason why we don't say nothing [sic] is because I don't want my child to grow up and they say, 'Well, they're not your real parents.' I don't want them hurting my child, because that is my child regardless whether it's donor or not. They're my child because I'm the one who raises it. That's my decision, my personal life." Here, Anita is emphasizing her role as social mother and fighting Euro-American notions that kinship is rooted in nature. In fact, nature is now "a site that can be thoroughly assisted by human intervention" (Gibbon and Novas 2008:3).

Patients worry about the stigmatization their child may face if it becomes public knowledge that the family is "abnormal." They have experienced the stigma of infertility, and they work hard to protect their children from any similar stigma. If couples have hidden the fact that they used an egg donor behind the cloak of their European vacation, then they will try to keep that fact hidden forever. Couples factor in the work and the money they spent in their efforts to build their families in making the decision whether or not to disclose to their children the fact of egg donation. Many couples discuss the fact that their children would not have been conceived without the hard work of intended parents (Strathern 2005:56). Claudia, of Seattle, said to me over a salad and appetizer we shared at a hip restaurant near Green Lake: "I don't want a lot of people to know about egg donation at this point. I went through a lot to have him, and I gave him life. I mean, I carried him, having him. It was not a good birth. We had some complications, because they induced me. Before, it was awesome, I had an awesome pregnancy." The logic seems to be that Claudia earned a right to motherhood through her many attempts to get pregnant and the difficult birth. She feels that disclosure of the fact that she used an egg donor would violate her claims of motherhood to her son. Thus, she hides the fact of donation.

I had met couples who did fit Dr. R.'s characterization of North Americans as "open." If a couple had been open about their infertility journey to the Czech Republic, then they tended to continue in their openness with their child. Diana, Petra's Czech coordinator, thought that it was pretty much half and half in terms of those who did and those who did not intend to tell their child they had been born of an egg donor. Hana claimed that 70 percent are in the no-tell camp. Thus, even among IVF brokers and doctors, there are different assumptions about North American patients. Nevertheless, clinicians do not seem to advise patients regarding disclosure. Within the virtual biosocial communities, those women who opt to disclose create separate threads from those who do not. These separate threads reveal different worldviews and assumptions about healthy parenting.

For those couples who do choose to disclose the fact of donation to their children, they must decide at what point they will tell their child (see also Nelson, Hertz, and Kramer 2013). A doctor in Prague said that for those who do intend to tell their children, they will probably wait until the children are twenty-five years old rather than telling them when they are young. Some North Americans I met are telling their children their conception stories when they are very small. Amazon sells books that can be individualized according to the method of conception and birth. Maria told me, "I did see some little books that explain how you were made. You can order them regular, all natural, or IVF. You can order them all kinds of ways, they're really cute." When I was following up with Linda and Michael, Linda showed me her book, which had been recommended by Maria, and explained:

> I tell them every day. Well, I shouldn't say every day. I found this great book. I read it to them; they have no clue. I tell them the story. I figure if I start now, by the time they do have a clue, they'll actually get it. I figure if I start now, they'll have it all engrained. I tell it as a fairy tale: *Mommy was your tummy big?* It's a story about the elephant and they go to the doctor. They have all these tests; she took all these medicines and no baby elephant; no baby came. You talk about the donor, a nice lady elephant with a beautiful hat, and she gives an egg. It's not the kind of egg you eat, because the baby asks that. No, this is a very special egg, and you put it together with daddy's cells and into mommy's tummy and it grows and it grows and it grows and that was you. So it's this really cool thing about donating.

In reading this book to her twins daily, Linda is attempting to normalize their conception. By normalizing their conception story through the reading of a fairy tale, she is giving her children a point for self-identification, to instill a healthy acceptance of egg donation.

Suzanne, the Canadian who did not seek out anonymous egg donation, was without a doubt that she would tell her daughter she was born of an egg donor. She did, however, worry that she did not have a lot of knowledge about the donor: "We'll definitely tell her, because everybody knows. So the chances of her finding out at some point are really quite high. For me, that's the biggest thing that I worry about now: How she's going to react when she finds out? Especially that we'll have to tell her that we don't know what her mother looked like or who she was or anything."

If parents do not disclose the conception story to their child, some problems can arise. A fertility doctor I spoke with in Prague described an interesting scenario:

I had maybe two years ago a very nice couple, they had egg donation and they contacted me shortly before delivery. The sister of the future mother had a three-year-old daughter with leukemia, and they asked their sister if the newborn could give blood for the transfusion. And they did not tell anyone that this is a donation child. They have agreed they will not tell anyone in the future that the child was conceived using donor eggs. But she loves her sister and a small child with leukemia. She was completely down. I don't know what was the result. She wanted to help, but she wanted to keep the secret, because of the child to be born. She didn't want to lose the good relationship with her sister. She phoned me a couple of times. This must be crazy.

Of course, such scenarios are unexpected and unanticipated. More and more often, they appear in popular movies such as *My Sister's Keeper, Delivery Man,* and *The Kids Are All Right.* They may or may not occur for the North Americans who are traveling this route to parenthood.

Scholars of international adoption have analyzed "heritage tours" that families take, during which adopted children are meant to identify with their ethnic roots by revisiting their homeland (F. Cohen 2015; see also Louie 2004). I was curious when following up with couples I knew from the Czech Republic about whether or not they envisioned similar tours for their families. I realized that those who were "open" about disclosure were also more open to the idea of returning to the Czech Republic on a quasi-"heritage" tour. Linda and Michael hope to bring their children to the Czech Republic once they can handle the travel. Diana, one of Petra's Czech-based coordinators, mused aloud to me over coffee, wondering why people would bring their children back:

One group wants to bring them back, which I don't really support and don't understand. I think there is no point. I know it's even hard for the women to carry the baby, which is her husband with some other girl. But they are easy with it. I [would] not tell the babies. Like when? Why? To which baby? Too soon, or too late. You can never know how they will act and you went through so much. The baby will tell you, "So you are not my mom actually." I will not tell. So I am more support[ive of] the group which is not to tell anybody.

Obviously, Diana concurs strongly with Dr. R. of the Zlín clinic. Indeed, Linda was a rare exception.

Overwhelmingly, couples did not see a need to bring their child or children back to the Czech Republic. Ben and Claudia, a couple who does not intend to disclose the fact of donation, fear that returning to the Czech Republic as a family could simply "open a can of worms." In order to maintain the secretive silence of having used egg donation, they will avoid returning to the Czech Republic once they have built the family they wanted.

Sustaining Community through Return Reproductive Tourism

Although couples who travel to the Czech Republic for IVF using egg donation do not anticipate taking any "heritage tours" later in their lives, they do often make several return trips to the Czech Republic for further cycles of IVF, successful or not. Thus, they are satisfied customers, appreciative of the vacation and the care they received, and impelled by others' or their own continued success stories. North American reproductive travelers have begun a trend that I suspect will only strengthen and continue into the future, which involves patients acting as consumers in a global marketplace of medicine. I argue that the "compulsive" element to these reproductive technologies is only extended by the reproductive travel industry. Now, couples not only feel compelled by the promise of technology but also keep feeling the need to return to the Czech Republic "to try once more." This compulsion is encouraged by the coordinators at the clinic, like Lenka, who say, "The only people who do not get pregnant are those who stop trying." Couples interpret this statement as a beacon of hope and do not critically step back and think about how the clinic is profiting from all their trips. They are propelled by the North American ideology of hard work. As patients interpret Czech doctors and nurses as compassionate, and low prices as a symbol of their empathy, they will not extend their legitimate critique of the North American "baby business" to the Czech context (Spar 2006).

Also, North Americans may have frozen embryos that they feel obligated to return to. Scholars such as Morgan (2009) have shown the weighty meanings North Americans invest in embryos. Because many North Americans believe that life begins at the moment of conception, embryos are imbricated with personhood. North America is very different from countries like the United Kingdom when it comes to stem cell research, which often uses embryos for laboratory research (Waldby and Mitchell 2006). In vitro fertilization generates "the embryo supply"; it is a "source of 'biolife'" (Franklin 2012:31). In the successful cases where an IVF cycle produces multiple embryos, couples must choose whether to freeze some of the embryos. In fact, most couples hope they will have embryos to freeze, since they see this as an investment in future family planning. If a couple returns to the Czech Republic for a cycle using frozen embryos, the woman will not have to go through egg retrieval again, easing her next cycle. However, if a couple ends up having twins, they may feel that their family is complete. In this case, they may face an ethical dilemma, also unanticipated, and be unsure of what to do with the remaining embryos in the Czech Republic. Just as the reality of raising multiples or the issue of disclosure may not be completely thought through, the existence of frozen embryos is another dilemma couples traveling this route to parenthood may face.

Julie, Faith's good friend who lived in South Carolina, had three children: twins from her first trip to the Czech Republic, and then an "oops" child conceived "naturally" after the birth of her twins. Despite the fact that she and her husband had three children, they felt that they had to go back for their embryos, which they had left at the clinic. Like some other women, Kate, of Florida, had a hard time thinking about destroying her embryos and planned to go back for them at some point. Some women, however, were blasé and were still uncertain whether they would return for their frozen embryos. In fact, the clinic coordinator, Ludmilla, admitted to me in the summer of 2014 that the clinic is now facing storage issues. She complained that many couples do not respond to the clinic's e-mails about their embryos. In response to this dilemma, the clinic has changed its contract so that it clearly states that it can destroy the embryos if the couple does not respond after a year of storage.

Late in the summer of 2012, after I had settled into my Texas apartment, I Skyped with Petra from IVF Choices. We spoke for well over an hour, and I could detect a significant shift in her disposition. She had been very chipper and positive when I met her two years previously, but I noticed that she now seemed tired and wary, both in her tone of voice and in her stronger criticism of her clients. The change may also have been due to the fact that she was raising two small children. As we spoke of the issue of frozen embryos, she said: "See, that's one thing that people don't realize. They're freezing their eggs. They're freezing their sperm. They're freezing their embryos. But eventually these could be human beings, and I don't think they think it through. They have all this stuff frozen and then they're afraid to use it, or they don't want to use it, and it's becoming a problem. I am glad that we don't have this problem, that we have the child that we wanted, and she's perfectly healthy." Because the reproductive travel industry is relatively new, the pioneers who travel this route are the first to face new dilemmas, often unanticipated in the initial compulsion to seek IVF, to transfer too many embryos, and to freeze too many embryos. Knowing that the frozen embryos exist, couples may feel compelled to return for continuous cycles, a situation that echoes the prodding of the technologies and clinical coordinators.

As North Americans continue to return to the Czech Republic, either for their frozen embryos or for fresh cycles, they keep in touch with one another in online communities. I also heard of couples coordinating future trips with each other so that they could meet once again in the Czech Republic. More than 50 percent of my sample traveled to the Czech Republic more than one time. Thus, a good number of reproductive tourists travel this route often.

Women Doing Kin Work

In addition to the common thread of return reproductive tourism, many couples maintain their social kinship bonds when they return home. "Families often go on meeting long after their children have arrived," which attests to the strength of the kinship bonds formed in the Czech Republic (Howell 2006:78). During her first trip in May 2008, Julie remembered ten or twelve couples "all coming or going." She explained, "We became very good friends with two of the couples we met over there, one from Georgia and one from Kentucky. We still get together with them a couple times a year." Faith, the wife of one of the couples she mentioned, joked:

We get together periodically with two other U.S. couples we met over in Zlín. We all had our egg retrievals done the same day, so our babies are all the same age. It's fun to keep in touch, and we have a lot in common because of infertility struggles and then having babies at the same time. One of the husbands likes to joke about the fact that our babies were all conceived in the same room on the same day. It makes people's heads turn, that's for sure. When we go out to eat together, we usually take up all the high chairs, and people ask us why the babies are all the same age, and which babies belong to what parents. There are three couples, but one set of twins, so four babies.

Even more interesting, one reproductive traveler's blog claimed that all offspring born from IVF in the Czech Republic must be related: "The last time we had to think about *anything* having to do with the procedure was the moment we stepped on the plane to Prague. It was as if we were on a private tour . . . but better, because we had three other couples undergoing IVF, and sharing the same experiences and nervousness. In a matter of a very few days we became friends—and probably friends for life. . . . It's as if any of the offspring born of the Czech experience shall be cousins!" Relationships established in the Czech clinic's waiting room, the pension, or online continue as patients disperse to their homes throughout North America. And the couples share a sense of relatedness, due to their common struggles, choices, experiences, and entrances to long-awaited parenthood.

Claudia and Ben kept in close contact with the couple they had first met, who also lived outside of Seattle. Four years after Claudia and her friend made their second trip together, the families were planning a summer trip to the beach. Some couples even celebrate major holidays together, such as Maria and Ryan, who host a family they had met. The fact that families choose to spend important holidays like Christmas with one another indicates the strength of social kinship bonds they have formed around similar family types.

Catherine Nash (2003) writes about Irish Americans who meet one another when they travel to Ireland to trace their genealogies. They initially meet online and then abroad in Ireland and often exchange gifts with one another. Nash characterizes their bonds as new geographies of relatedness. Similarly, I see the commonality and affinity of shared experiences of infertility and going through a cycle of in vitro fertilization in the Czech Republic as creating new forms of relatedness. These bonds, as with the Irish Americans described by Nash, are sustained virtually and literally. The virtual biosocial communities women entered when diagnosed with infertility continue to thrive. Faith even claimed that her participation in social media has saved her life and ensured that she does not suffer isolation as she raises her three children.

Just as the virtual biosocial communities for infertility support groups were gendered, these communities continue to be populated largely by women who continue performing "kinship work" (di Leonardo 1987) by keeping in touch with former hosts, brokers, and fellow patients. Maria admitted she sent Christmas cards, saying, "Yeah we definitely [send] Christmas cards. You know, everybody's got to get updated pictures and all that good stuff." She continued, "I usually talk on the phone with Janice because it just seems to be easier for them, because they're not big on the computer. With Linda and Michael, it's usually e-mail, because you know they are busy, they were busy before they had twins." Women sustain the social kinship bonds that were built online and in the Czech Republic. This reinscribes the gendered nature of reproduction and infertility, as women continue to populate these Internet communities, advising and supporting one another.

North American reproductive travelers not only stay in touch with one another but also update the clinic with news of a successful cycle and send updates to brokers and Mareka at the pension. Dr. M. said that about 70 percent of the clinic's North American patients send pictures of their babies that could become part of the typical baby wall. These photographs become testimonials to the clinic's success and encourage future business. Maria also keeps in touch with Mareka. She told me, "Mareka gets pictures at Christmastime, cards. The last time we were there, she gave us bibs that say 'Made in Zlín,' and they were so cute. When you're there, it's just like you're family, and it makes all the difference in the world." Maria continued, "We're talking about going back, not for a kid, but for a visit. We want to see Mareka." Other women became close to their Czech coordinators, those who showed them the town or provided transportation to the clinic. Some patients sent gifts to Czech coordinators or, more commonly, became Facebook friends. Jana was a bubbly coordinator who worked for Petra in Brno. She admitted she joined Facebook so she could keep in touch with two couples in particular. After Jana gave birth to her own daughter, she was stunned to receive a huge box full of clothes from one of her previous patients. These gifts reinforce social kinship ties that are central connections sustaining reproductive travel from North America to the Czech Republic.

Although North American couples disperse to their homes all over the country upon returning from their fertility holidays in the Czech Republic, they also remain strongly connected. Women maintain relationships with other women they have met within various biosocial virtual communities—women they have met in the Czech Republic, women who had embryo transfers at the same time, and IVF brokers and/or coordinators. These virtual and real biosocial communities are composed of women who are now lay experts in the world of reproductive technologies. As women face unexpected ethical dilemmas such as whether to disclose or what to do with frozen embryos, they advise and support one another. As with the virtual communities created by infertility support websites described in chapter 2, the communities that are sustained by North American reproductive travelers also may shift with time, but they remain a central part of these families' lives.

North Americans who travel to the Czech Republic to undergo IVF using an egg donor do not always go home with the best kind of "souvenirs." Some couples find themselves turning to the adoption route after another miscarriage, as Valerie and Dan did. Some will find themselves fostering and then adopting three beautiful boys, as Lauren and John did. Some will return to the Czech Republic repeatedly, while others will go back to the expensively decorated clinics in their North American cities, realizing that it is actually a lot of work to travel to the Czech Republic for IVF.

Whether women are raising multiples or singles, children whom they themselves bore or not, they keep in touch with one another and their compassionate hosts in the Czech Republic. I, too, maintain contact with many of the women I met during the course of my research. I joyfully watch via Facebook as their children grow, amazed at how quickly they change and at all the shenanigans they can get into. We remain connected, despite being spread out across North America.

Conclusion

An Eye to the Future

I had finally moved to Texas and was settling into my new apartment and position at the University of Texas, Arlington. I was looking forward to catching up with my last couple, Allan and Alida. Luckily for me, they lived outside of Austin, just a three-hour drive away. Alida was kind enough to invite me to stay with them for the Labor Day weekend, and I was looking forward to exploring the capital of Texas.

When I initially e-mailed Alida to follow up with her, I had no idea whether they had been successful, whether they had come home from the Czech Republic with the best possible souvenir. We had not spoken since the last day I was in Zlín in the summer of 2011. In our first e-mail exchange, she mentioned that her schedule was restricted in terms of the days she could meet because her daughter was going through a lot of therapy. I quickly learned that Alida had had a baby girl, but the baby's beginning was a treacherous, difficult one. My excitement soon turned to dread.

Alida greeted me on a sunny Saturday afternoon, out of breath, her long brown hair haphazardly arranged on top of her head. I felt guilty that she had been busy cleaning in anticipation of my arrival. I had purposely avoided coming at lunch so that they would not feel obligated to feed me. Of course, this trick failed, since Allan had apparently driven an hour and a half away to pick up the best-known Texas barbeque.

I quickly realized the dark reality that comes with premature birth, which greeted me immediately upon entering their suburban home. The dimly lit living room hummed, and an oxygen tank steadily pumped in the corner, marking time, as I found a seat on a large, overstuffed sofa. Alida perched on one of two armchairs across from me, while a large television featuring a cooking show flickered in the background. It was immediately apparent that Alida spent most of her days with her premature daughter Sandra, given the contents of her loquacious conversation. She would ask me a question, but then quickly start bringing me up to date on her life. She introduced me to her extremely tiny daughter, Sandra, whose forehead was encircled with oxygen tubes. I did not even reach out my arms to hold her, nervous about the tubes and the frailty of her body.

Alida poured out her story to me in fits, in between cleaning, preparing the table for the delicious brisket that was en route to us, and feeding Sandra and changing her diaper. She moved back and forth from the kitchen behind me to the living room, often turning the lights on and off. I could tell she usually kept the lights off, but she also saw that I would need more light for taking notes as she brought me up to date with what had happened.

Alida had gotten pregnant on her first trip to the Czech Republic in the winter of 2009, but she had miscarried twins. She was again successfully pregnant with twins from her cycle in the summer of 2011, yet she miscarried the male twin she had planned to name Danny in October. However, she was advised to keep the placenta inside, or else she would lose her daughter as well. She had a cerclage (a surgical procedure also known as a cervical stitch in which the cervix is sewn closed) done at five months, which led to incontinence and her body shutting down. Alida delivered Sandra on December 27, at her twenty-fifth week—the "survival" week. However, Sandra had to stay in the hospital NICU for five more months. Despite her pain, Alida did not tell people she had conceived. She remembered how her friends had thrown her a baby shower the first time she had gotten pregnant, and that it had been so sad for her after she miscarried. Once again, she shrouded herself in silence. When I had met Alida and Allan in the Czech Republic, she had said that she relished the fact that they had the opportunity to have children without going into debt. Ironically, they now faced mounds of debt from the hospital bills.

Next to Alida, a large oxygen tank that breathed and droned regularly in the background sat in the way in their already cramped living room. There were boxes of special formula for their daughter, whose digestive system was not yet adequately developed. Even determining her age was difficult because she had been born so prematurely; they were not sure whether to count from her due date or the actual date of birth. Alida and Allan faced many battles with insurance, as they worried about huge hospital bills. While Alida dreamily thought she would like to return to the Czech Republic just "one more time," Allan was dog tired and steadfast in saying no; there was absolutely no way he could go through anything resembling their experience again.

Complications

Alida and Allan's story is the saddest that I have encountered, and I have encountered many painful moments with couples that I foolishly did not anticipate. A study from 2002 found that children conceived with ICSI and IVF are twice as likely to have a major birth defect (Spar and Harrington 2009:57). Furthermore, there is a 30 percent rate of multiple pregnancies with the use of ARTs, which can also mean societal costs. There is "no central record of multiple births following the use of fertility drugs" (Price 1999:50). Patients like Allan and Alida who cross borders for fertility treatment may return home needing more care.

There are obvious repercussions when reproductive medicine is unregulated. In addition to the basic inequity of access to reproductive technologies in the United States, women are trying to make cost-effective decisions about embryo transfers without considering their own health—since multiple births may lead to miscarriage or premature birth. These complications put stress and strain on the health care system. In addition, because these "hope technologies" can be compelling, couples may be spending beyond their means when trying to have a family.

Even though couples save money by traveling to the Czech Republic rather than undergoing IVF in North America, many are still stretching their finances beyond what they can manage, spending beyond their means and possibly jeopardizing their family's welfare with debt. Couples have remortgaged their houses, spent their savings, and paid for their trips with high-interest credit cards. They are often willing to spend what is necessary to build a family and claim that they can make more money. As Linda panicked about adding on to the house, she knew that they had spent their savings, and this contributed to the worry over the needed renovations. Couples sometimes become financially strapped. Faith spoke often of her husband working three jobs so that they could make another trip to the Czech Republic to have more children.

These couples' experiences illuminate the need to acknowledge that this is a market that entails commercial transactions, a discussion that has largely been taboo thus far (Spar and Harrington 2009). There needs to be an acknowledgment that the market is now global, extending to Thailand, the Czech Republic, India, South Africa, and beyond. Major issues related to the market of reproductive technologies in the United States include price, inequity, absence of property rights, health risks, and potential societal costs (Spar and Harrington 2009:49). Many of these issues stem from a lack of conversation about questions such as the legal status of the embryo, the right to procreate using reproductive technologies, and contract enforceability in relation to reproductive technologies. However, the largest issue I foresee for the families built via fertility holidays in the Czech Republic relates to personal rights to information for the children born via anonymous egg donor. Even further, I foresee discourses about "rights" of children gaining momentum as the children born of ARTs reach an age at which they may wish to seek information about their genetic parentage. A major question for the future is the extent to which the children born via IVF in the Czech Republic will learn about their origins, and how they will react to that knowledge. Much as their parents did when suffering infertility, will they turn to the Internet in search of their gamete donors?

As the children born via IVF using egg donation grow older, if they are told about the facts of their conception, there may be an initiative on their part to push for open donation in the Czech Republic. As I listen to a story on National Public Radio about a girl who wrote letters to a hundred of her mother's classmates, seeking out her biological father, it seems likely that the weight given to biology by children may also arise for the children of those couples I met in the Czech Republic. It is important to monitor their futures and to anticipate ethical dilemmas these families may continue to confront. For the time being, couples will continue to travel to the Czech Republic for IVF as more people learn about this possible route to parenthood.

Fertility Holidays as Contradiction

This book has traced North American reproductive journeys to the Czech Republic for in vitro fertilization, often for couples using egg donation. Throughout each leg of these journeys, it has underscored the complex contradictions and ambiguities with which patient tourists must grapple as they make decisions as consumers in a global marketplace of reproductive technologies. In addition, it has revealed the gendered nature of reproductive travel as women propel most fertility journeys abroad. Women actively participate in virtual biosocial communities where they learn about Czech fertility holidays. Upon returning home, women are frequently the ones to continue the kin work of sustaining social kinship bonds that were built in the Czech Republic.

This book contributes to the burgeoning scholarship on reproductive travel. By offering an intimate account of the lives of North Americans who embark on fertility holidays to the Czech Republic, it has painted the culturally specific ways in which lower-middle-class North American women respond to their infertility. They often assume proactive roles and turn to the Internet seeking more options than those that are too costly in North America. In the global marketplace of reproductive tourism destinations, couples make decisions as patient-consumers who are fed up with the greed and lack of care from North American fertility specialists. Goaded by imaginations of a white Central European egg donor, a European vacation, and doctors who care, women become embroiled in and embody contradictory experiences when they try to treat their fertility journeys as vacations. Fertility holidays, as "diasporas of hope," extend the hope entangled within the promise of reproductive technologies. The reproductive tourism industry will continue to grow as neoliberal health care policies expand globally. Patients are now consumers shopping in a global marketplace of medical care. They must weigh new kinds of risks as they assume increasing responsibility for their own health care.

I began by exploring lower-middle-class couples' first realization of their infertility and how American notions of hard work and positive thinking imbue their responses. They confront infertility with a moral axiom to be healthy, both emotionally and physically. Besides suffering from the emotional pain that accompanies infertility, women suffer additional layers of stigma and often shoulder their pain secretly. They quickly grow wary of profit-seeking doctors who lack compassion. Feeling nickel-and-dimed at each stage of treatment, they are barred from accessing readily available technologies at home because of the steep costs. Filled with despair, they begin to conduct online searches for support, information, and other opportunities for creating a family. On a recent episode of the television comedy *Veep*, Jonah, the political aide everyone loves to hate, is ridiculed for his research skills when a man asks him sardonically, "So you Googled it?" But it is vital that anthropologists pay more attention to the Internet and the role it plays in the lives of patients who suffer various problems. The Internet has become the main resource used by patients acting as diligent consumers of medical services. It is also where new kinds of communities are being built among patients who can share in their suffering with others facing the same issues.

Having access to information online is generally deemed to be empowering for patient-consumers. Women feel buoyed by the support they receive from others in various virtual support groups; they encourage one another to never give up. They feel empowered by the amount of information they can learn as they navigate the world of assisted reproduction. Despite the positive associations patients attribute to and experience in their usage of the Internet, the fact remains that patients are unquestioningly accepting personal responsibility for their health care. Even more problematic, they must manage the risks associated with traveling abroad for IVF. They must be diligent consumers in a vast global marketplace.

The Internet is also a global marketplace for the production of new types of medical holidays. "Fertility holidays" created by IVF brokers in North America for trips to the Czech Republic and their fertility holiday websites must be considered political economies of hope, whereby patients who want to create particular kinds of families are also promised European vacations and clinical experiences where doctors truly care. The convergence of biosocial communities of patient groups, along with the creation of new types of vacations, builds on the imaginations, fantasies, and hopes of infertile women. The Internet is where gendered reproductive mobilities begin.

This book has framed the services provided by IVF brokers, Czech clinicians, and hosts as "intimate labor" that is central to the success of the Czech reproductive tourism industry. Care is a central component of medical service in a global medical tourism market. Just as patients must be diligent consumers, health care providers are also service providers. They must be attuned to the demands of different groups of patients, continually expanding their market to new groups. The intimate labor that has been provided by IVF brokers, Czech coordinators, hosts, and doctors cannot be underestimated. It is the intimate labor of Czech hosts that is central to the structures of the global economy of the travel and medical industry. The brokers assume much of the stress that is associated with being a consumer in a global marketplace. Furthermore, they play upon North American dissatisfaction with the profit-driven baby business in the States.

The Czech Republic is an important "hub" in the global reproductive medical marketplace, particularly because it offers anonymous gamete donation. For those pioneers who first ventured along this reproductive travel route, IVF brokers played a large role in coordinating various parts of their journeys, down to the intimate clinical encounter. However, Czech clinics have increasingly usurped the role of the broker by hiring their own coordinators to deal with patients directly. At the same time, patients are becoming consumer activists in encouraging one another to "do it themselves." For the most part, IVF brokers have been ousted from the reproductive tourism industry. Czech clinics have grown savvy in employing the discourse of hard work and positive thinking that compels North Americans to keep returning. However, North American patients often turn a blind eye to the profit motives of Czech clinicians and coordinators.

It is while patients are in the Czech Republic that the biosocial communities formed online materialize, as patients meet one another over the course of their treatment. The North American patients form strong social kinship bonds with one another as they retreat into the anonymity of staying at a pension in a small Moravian town. These communities continue to grow and become founts of support for women when they return home, perhaps to find themselves pregnant with multiples or facing another failed cycle. The social kinship bonds are sustained via social media and holiday visits and trips, either in North America or back to the Czech Republic.

The ultimate contradiction, I argue, for North American reproductive travelers going to the Czech Republic in order to create a family is that they really do try to embody an idealized tourist while they are in the Czech Republic. In attempting to treat their journeys as a vacation, they are internalizing the notion that they must be emotionally healthy and stress free during their IVF cycle. But despite their best intentions, their vacations are ultimately interrupted by the reality of their journeys. Nevertheless, they will return home and paint pictures through more testimonials that they truly did have a "fertility holiday."

NOTES

INTRODUCTION

1 This is a procedure whereby a single sperm is injected directly into the egg.

2 On a happier note, April and Larry were successful the following year with a second round of IVF.

3 I have used pseudonyms for all my informants. Given the sensitive nature of infertility, I did not always hear back from reproductive travelers whom I met in the Czech Republic. I have assumed that they were unsuccessful or that they wanted to distance themselves from their experiences in the Czech Republic.

4 In asking informants their occupation, in visiting their homes, and through interviews and conversations, I have ascertained that most of them fall within the lower middle class, as defined by sociological models based on education and income. The lower middle class, also referred to as the working class, is "composed of low-skill manual workers, clerical workers, and retail salespeople" (Gilbert 2008:252). Lower-middle-class household incomes range from $35,000 to $75,000 (Thompson and Hickey 2005). I suspect that two couples from my sample fall into the working class, whose income ranges between $16,000 and $30,000 (Thompson and Hickey 2005). Two couples from my sample were of the upper middle class, which consists of "well-paid, university trained managers and professionals" (Gilbert 2008:251).

CHAPTER 1. FROM HOPE TO ALIENATION

1 It must be noted that their treatments have not been successful, so this may color their consideration of the U.S. baby business. However, I do not wish to discredit their complaints.

2 More than 1 million Americans underwent some form of fertility treatment in 2004 (Spar 2006)

3 In this procedure, fertilized eggs are cultured for a period of five days before they are implanted into the uterus, which improves the success rates of IVF.

4 Typically, a round of IVF can cost $10,000 to $15,000. With an egg donor, the price increases to $30,000. With a surrogate, it can rise to $90,000. These numbers are based on prices quoted by patient and physician informants of this study.

5 She is referring to a "chemical pregnancy"—a very early miscarriage.

6 If a woman's first IVF cycle successfully produces multiple embryos, she can freeze the embryos for a future cycle. Although the success rate is lower with frozen embryos, the woman does not have to undergo medication and egg retrieval.

CHAPTER 2. VIRTUAL COMMUNITIES AND MARKETS

1 One in three American adults has gone online to learn more about a medical condition (Fox and Duggan 2013).
2 Throsby (2004:7) writes that almost 80 percent of all cycles started do not result in a live birth.

CHAPTER 3. INTIMATE LABOR WITHIN CZECH CLINICS

1 For a sense of comparison, slightly more than 1.5 percent of all births in the United States are born via ARTs. One reason for the higher percentage in the Czech Republic is that most Czech women using IVF are younger than thirty-five, which means there is a higher success rate of live births.
2 "Gamete" is the biological term for a sexual reproduction cell, such as a sperm or an ovum.
3 See http://www.stopneplodnosti.cz.
4 There may be a difference between Canadian and American patients, since legal regulations differ between the two countries. Because gamete donation must be open in Canada, patients like Suzanne may have this preference.
5 While North Americans assumed Lenka matched donors and recipients, this was actually under the purview of the doctor.
6 North American clients implicitly assume that Czech women at the clinic act only as donors and not as potential patients.

BIBLIOGRAPHY

Abadie, Roberto. 2010. *The Professional Guinea Pig: Big Pharma and the Risky World of Human Subjects*. Durham, NC: Duke University Press.

Abu-Lughod, Lila. 1990. "The Romance of Resistance: Tracing Transformations of Power through Bedouin Women." *American Ethnologist* 17(1):41–55.

Almeling, Rene. 2006. "'Why Do You Want to Be a Donor?': Gender and the Production of Altruism in Egg and Sperm Donation." *New Genetics and Society* 25(2):143–157.

———. 2007. "Selling Genes, Selling Gender: Egg Agencies, Sperm Banks, and the Medical Market in Genetic Materials." *American Sociological Review* 72(3):319–340.

Anagnost, Ann. 2004. "Maternal Labor in a Transnational Circuit." Pp. 139–167 in *Consuming Motherhood*, edited by Janelle S. Taylor, Linda L. Layne, and Danielle F. Wozniak. New Brunswick, NJ: Rutgers University Press.

Appadurai, Arjun. 1996. *Modernity at Large: Cultural Dimensions of Globalization*. Minneapolis: University of Minnesota Press.

Becker, Gay. 2000. *The Elusive Embryo: How Men and Women Approach New Reproductive Technologies*. Berkeley: University of California Press.

Bell, Ann V. 2009. "'It's Way Out of My League': Low-Income Women's Experiences of Medicalized Infertility." *Gender and Society* 23(5):688–709.

Bergmann, Sven. 2011. "Reproductive Agency and Projects: Germans Searching for Egg Donation in Spain and the Czech Republic." *Reproductive BioMedicine Online* 23(5):600–608.

———. 2012. "Resemblance That Matters: On Transnational Anonymized Egg Donation in Two European IVF Clinics." Pp. 331–355 in *Reproductive Technologies as Global Form: Ethnographies of Knowledge, Practices, and Transnational Encounters*, edited by Michi Knecht, Maren Klotz, and Stefan Beck. Frankfurt: Campus Verlag.

Bharadwaj, Aditya. 2008. "Biosociality and Biocrossings: Encounters with Assisted Conception and Embryonic Stem Cells in India." Pp. 98–116 in *Biosocialities, Genetics and the Social Sciences: Making Biologies and Identities*, edited by Sarah Gibbon and Carlos Novas. New York: Routledge.

Blumhagen, Dan. 2009. "The Doctor's White Coat: The Image of the Physician in Modern America." Pp. 111–116 in *Understanding and Applying Medical Anthropology*, edited by Peter Brown and Ron Barrett. 2nd ed. New York: McGraw-Hill.

Blyth, Eric, and Abigail Farrand. 2005. "Reproductive Tourism: A Price Worth Paying for Reproductive Autonomy?" *Critical Social Policy* 25(1):91–114.

Boris, Eileen, and Rhacel Salazar Parreñas. 2010. "Introduction." Pp. 1–12 in *Intimate Labors: Cultures, Technologies, and the Politics of Care*, edited by Eileen Boris and Rhacel Salazar Parreñas. Stanford, CA: Stanford University Press.

Briggs, Laura. 2010. "Foreign and Domestic: Adoption, Immigration, and Privatization." Pp. 49–62 in *Intimate Labors: Cultures, Technologies, and the Politics of Care*, edited by Eileen Boris and Rhacel Salazar Parreñas. Stanford, CA: Stanford University Press.

Cabezas, Amalia L. 2011. "Intimate Encounters: Affective Economies in Cuba and the Dominican Republic." *European Review of Latin American and Caribbean Studies* 91:3–14.

Cahn, Naomi. 2013. *The New Kinship: Constructing Donor-Conceived Families*. New York: NYU Press.

Chibnik, Michael. 2011. *Anthropology, Economics, and Choice*. Austin: University of Texas Press.

Clarke, Adele E., Janet K. Shim, Laura Mamo, Jennifer Ruth Fosket, and Jennifer R. Fishman. 2003. "Biomedicalization: Technoscientific Transformations of Health, Illness, and U.S. Biomedicine." *American Sociological Review* 68(2):161–194.

Cohen, Frayda. 2015. "Tracing the Red Thread: Chinese-U.S. Transnational Adoption and the Legacies of 'Home.'" *Anthropologica* 57(1):41–52.

Cohen, Lawrence. 2002. "The Other Kidney: Biopolitics beyond Recognition." Pp. 9–30 in *Commodifying Bodies*, edited by Nancy Scheper-Hughes and Loïc Wacant. London: Sage.

Colen, Shellee. 1986. "'With Respect and Feelings': Voices of West Indian Childcare and Domestic Workers in New York City." Pp. 46–70 in *All American Women: Lines That Divide, Ties That Blind*, edited by Johnnetta B. Cole. New York: Free Press.

Crouch, David, Rhona Jackson, and Felix Thompson, eds. 2005. *The Media and the Tourist Imagination: Converging Cultures*. New York: Routledge.

Davis-Floyd, Robbie. 2003. *Birth as an American Rite of Passage*. 2nd ed. Berkeley: University of California Press.

Deomampo, Daisy. 2013. "Transnational Surrogacy in India: Interrogating Power and Women's Agency." *Frontiers: A Journal of Women's Studies* 34(3):167–188.

di Leonardo, Micaela. 1987. "The Female World of Cards and Holidays: Women, Families, and Kinship." *Signs* 12(3):440–453.

Ducey, Ariel. 2010. "Technologies of Caring Labor: From Objects to Affect." Pp. 18–32 in *Intimate Labors: Cultures, Technologies, and the Politics of Care*, edited by Eileen Boris and Rhacel Salazar Parreñas. Stanford, CA: Stanford University Press.

Duggan Maeve, and Aaron Smith. 2013. *Cell Internet Use 2013*. Washington, DC: Pew Research Center.

Ehrenreich, Barbara. 2009. *Bright-Sided: How Positive Thinking Is Undermining America*. New York: Metropolitan Books.

Fox, Susannah, and Maeve Duggan. 2013. "Health Online 2013." http://www.pewinternet.org/2013/01/15/health-online-2013/.

Franklin, Sarah. 1997a. *Embodied Progress: A Cultural Account of Assisted Conception.* London: Routledge.

———. 1997b. "Making Sense of Missed Conceptions: Anthropological Perspectives on Unexplained Infertility." Pp. 99–109 in *Situated Lives: Gender and Culture in Everyday Life,* edited by Louise Lamphere, Helena Ragoné, and Patricia Zavella. New York: Routledge.

———. 2012. "Five Million Miracle Babies Later: The Biocultural Legacies of IVF." Pp. 27–60 in *Reproductive Technologies as Global Form: Ethnographies of Knowledge, Practices, and Transnational Encounters,* edited by Michi Knecht, Maren Klotz, and Stefan Beck. Frankfurt: Campus Verlag.

———. 2013. *Biological Relatives: IVF, Stem Cells, and the Future of Kinship.* Durham, NC: Duke University Press.

Frohlick, Susan. 2015. "'Souvenir Babies' and Abandoned Homes: Tracking the Reproductive Forces of Tourism." *Anthropologica* 57(1):63–76.

Gibbon, Sarah, and Carlos Novas. 2008. "Introduction: Biosocialities, Genetics and the Social Sciences." Pp. 1–18 in *Biosocialities, Genetics and the Social Sciences: Making Biologies and Identities,* edited by Sarah Gibbon and Carlos Novas. New York: Routledge.

Gilbert, Dennis. 2008. *The American Class Structure in an Age of Growing Inequality.* 7th ed. Belmont, CA: Wadsworth.

Ginsburg, Faye, and Rayna Rapp, eds. 1995a. *Conceiving the New World Order: The Global Politics of Reproduction.* Berkeley: University of California Press.

———. 1995b. "Introduction." Pp. 1–7 in *Conceiving the New World Order: The Global Politics of Reproduction,* edited by Faye Ginsburg and Rayna Rapp. Berkeley: University of California Press.

Global IVF. 2012. "Views about Gestational Surrogacy from around the World." Accessed April 2, 2014. http://globalivf.com/2012/09/05/different-views-about-gestational-surrogacy/ surrogacy/.

Goffman, Irving. 1963. *Stigma: Notes on the Management of Spoiled Identity.* New York: Simon and Schuster.

Greil, Arthur L., and Julia McQuillan. 2010. "'Trying' Times: Medicalization, Intent, and Ambiguity in the Definition of Infertility." *Medical Anthropology Quarterly* 24(2):137–156.

Guell, Cornelia 2012. "Self-Care at the Margins: Meals and Meters in Migrants' Diabetes Tactics." *Medical Anthropology Quarterly* 26(4):518–533.

Gürtin, Zeynep B. 2012. "Practitioners as Interface Agents between the Local and the Global: The Localization of IVF in Turkey." Pp. 81–110 in *Reproductive Technologies as Global Form: Ethnographies of Knowledge, Practices, and Transnational Encounters,* edited by Michi Knecht, Maren Klotz, and Stefan Beck. Frankfurt: Campus Verlag.

Gürtin, Zeynep, and Marcia Inhorn. 2011 "Introduction: Travelling for Conception and the Global Assisted Reproduction Market." *Reproductive BioMedicine Online* 23(5):535–537.

Heng, Boon Chin. 2006. "'Reproductive Tourism': Should Locally Registered Fertility Doctors Be Held Accountable for Channeling Patients to Foreign Medical Establishments?" *Human Reproduction* 21(3):840–842.

———. 2007. "Regulatory Safeguards Needed for the Traveling Foreign Egg Donor." *Human Reproduction* 22(8):2350–2352.

Hertz, Rosanna. 2006. *Single by Chance, Mothers by Choice: How Women Are Choosing Parenthood without Marriage and Creating the New American Family*. New York: Oxford University Press.

Horton, Sarah, Cesar Abadia, Jessica Mulligan, and Jennifer Jo Thompson. 2014. "Critical Anthropology of Global Health 'Take a Stand' Statement: A Critical Medical Anthropological Approach to the U.S.'s Affordable Care Act." *Medical Anthropology Quarterly* 28(1):1–22.

Howell, Signe. 2006. *Kinning of Foreigners: Transnational Adoption in a Global Perspective*. New York: Berghahn Books.

Inhorn, Marcia. 1994. *Quest for Conception: Gender, Infertility and Egyptian Medical Traditions*. Philadelphia: University of Pennsylvania Press.

———. 2003. *Local Babies, Global Science: Gender, Religion and in Vitro Fertilization in Egypt*. New York: Routledge.

———. 2004. "Privacy, Privatization, and the Politics of Patronage: Ethnographic Challenges to Penetrating the Secret World of Middle Eastern, Hospital-Based In Vitro Fertilization." *Social Science and Medicine* 59(10):2095–2108.

———. 2011. "Diasporic Dreaming: 'Return Reproductive Tourism' to the Middle East." *Reproductive BioMedicine Online* 23(5):582–591.

———. 2012. *The New Arab Man: Emergent Masculinities, Technologies, and Islam in the Middle East*. Princeton, NJ: Princeton University Press.

Inhorn, Marcia C., and Daphna Birenbaum-Carmeli. 2008. "Assisted Reproductive Technologies and Culture Change." *Annual Review of Anthropology* 37:177–196.

Inhorn, Marcia, and Pasquale Patrizio. 2009. "Rethinking Reproductive 'Tourism' as Reproductive 'Exile.'" *Fertility and Sterility* 92(3):904–906.

———. 2012. "The Global Landscape of Cross-Border Reproductive Care: Twenty Key Findings for the New Millennium." *Current Opinion in Obstetrics and Gynecology* 24(3):158–163.

Jacobson, Heather. 2008. *Culture Keeping: White Mothers, International Adoption, and the Negotiation of Family Difference*. Nashville, TN: Vanderbilt University Press.

———. 2009. "Interracial Surveillance and Biological Privilege: Adoptive Families in the Public Eye." Pp. 73–93 in *Who's Watching? Daily Practices of Surveillance among Contemporary Families*, edited by Margaret K. Nelson and Anita Ilta Garey. Nashville, TN: Vanderbilt University Press.

Janzen, John M. 1982. *The Quest for Therapy: Medical Pluralism in Lower Zaire*. Berkeley: University of California Press.

Josefsson, Ulrika. 2006. "Patients' Online Information-Seeking Behavior." Pp. 127–147 in *The Internet and Health Care: Theory, Research, and Practice*, edited by Monica Murero and Ronald Price. Mahwah, NJ: Erlbaum.

Kahn, Susan Martha. 2000. *Reproducing Jews: A Cultural Account of Assisted Conception in Israel*. Durham, NC: Duke University Press.

Kimbrell, Andrew. 1993. *The Human Body Shop: The Engineering and Marketing of Life*. San Francisco: Harper.

Kleinman, Arthur. 1980. *Patients and Healers in the Context of Culture: An Exploration of the Borderland between Anthropology, Medicine, and Psychiatry*. Berkeley: University of California Press.

Klotz, Maren. 2012. "Making Connections: Reflecting on Trains, Kinship and Information Technology." Pp. 111–138 in *Reproductive Technologies as Global Form: Ethnographies of Knowledge, Practices, and Transnational Encounters*, edited by Michi Knecht, Maren Klotz, and Stefan Beck. Frankfurt: Campus Verlag.

Klotz, Maren, and Michi Knecht. 2012. "What Is Europeanization in the Field of Assisted Reproductive Technologies?" Pp. 283–305 in *Reproductive Technologies as Global Form: Ethnographies of Knowledge, Practices, and Transnational Encounters*, edited by Michi Knecht, Maren Klotz, and Stefan Beck. Frankfurt: Campus Verlag.

Knecht, Michi, Maren Klotz, and Stefan Beck. 2012. "Reproductive Technologies as Global Form: Introduction." Pp. 11–26 in *Reproductive Technologies as Global Form: Ethnographies of Knowledge, Practices, and Transnational Encounters*, edited by Michi Knecht, Maren Klotz, and Stefan Beck. Frankfurt: Campus Verlag.

Knoll, Eva-Maria. 2001. "Reproduktionsmedizinische Imaginationen. Überlegungen zum österreichischen IVF-Diskurs aus ethnologisch-feministischer Perspektive." Master's thesis, University of Vienna.

———. 2012. "Reproducing Hungarians: Reflections on Fuzzy Boundaries in Reproductive Border Crossing." Pp. 255–282 in *Reproductive Technologies as Global Form: Ethnographies of Knowledge, Practices, and Transnational Encounters*, edited by Michi Knecht, Maren Klotz, and Stefan Beck. Frankfurt: Campus Verlag.

Konrad, Monica. 2005. *Narrating the New Predictive Genetics: Ethics, Ethnography and Science*. Cambridge: Cambridge University Press.

Kottak, Conrad Phillip. 2011. *Mirror for Humanity: A Concise Introduction to Cultural Anthropology*. 8th ed. Boston: McGraw-Hill.

Layne, Linda. 2003. *Motherhood Lost: A Feminist Account of Pregnancy Loss in America*. New York: Routledge.

Lee, Sandra Soo-Jin. 2013. "Race, Risk, and Recreation in Personal Genomics: The Limits of Play." *Medical Anthropology Quarterly* 27(4):550–569.

Levine, Nancy E. 2008. "Alternative Kinship, Marriage, and Reproduction." *Annual Review of Anthropology* 37:375–389.

Löfgren, Orvar. 1999. *On Holiday: A History of Vacationing*. Berkeley: University of California Press.

Louie, Andrea. 2004. *Chineseness across Borders: Renegotiating Chinese Identities in China and the United States*. Durham, NC: Duke University Press.

Lupton, Deborah. 1999. "Risk and the Ontology of Pregnant Embodiment." Pp. 59–85 in *Risk and Sociocultural Theory: New Directions and Perspectives*, edited by Deborah Lupton. Cambridge: Cambridge University Press.

Martin, Emily. 1989. *The Woman in the Body: A Cultural Analysis of Reproduction.* Boston: Beacon Press.

Matorras, Roberto. 2005. "Reproductive Exile versus Reproductive Tourism." *Human Reproduction* 20(12):3571.

Metzl, Jonathan M., and Anna Kirkland, eds. 2010. *Against Health: How Health Became the New Morality.* New York: NYU Press.

Mol, Annemarie. 2008. *The Logic of Care: Health and the Problem of Patient Choice.* New York: Routledge.

Morgan, Lynn M. 2009. *Icons of Life: A Cultural History of Human Embryos.* Berkeley: University of California Press.

Nahar, Papreen, and Sjaak van der Geest. 2014. "How Women in Bangladesh Confront the Stigma of Childlessness: Agency, Resilience, and Resistance." *Medical Anthropology Quarterly* 28(3):381–398.

Nahman, Michael. 2008. "Nodes of Desire: Romanian Egg Sellers, 'Dignity' and Feminist Alliances in Transnational Ova Exchanges." *European Journal of Women's Studies* 15(2):65–82.

———. 2013. *Extractions: An Ethnography of Reproductive Tourism.* London: Palgrave Macmillan.

Nash, Catherine. 2003. "'They're Family!': Cultural Geographies of Relatedness in Popular Genealogy." Pp. 179–203 in *Uprootings/Regroundings: Questions of Home and Migration,* edited by Sara Ahmed, Claudia Castañeda, and Anne-Marie Fortie. Oxford: Berg.

Nelson, Margaret K., Rosanna Hertz, and Wendy Kramer. 2013. "Making Sense of Donors and Donor Siblings: A Comparison of the Perceptions of Donor-Conceived Offspring in Lesbian-Parent and Heterosexual Parent Families." Pp. 1–42 in *Visions of the 21st Century Family: Transforming Structure and Identities,* edited by Patricia Neff Claster and Sampson Lee Blair. Bingley, UK: Emerald Group.

Nygren, Karl, David Adamson, Fernando Zegers-Hochschild, Jacques de Mouzon, and International Committee Monitoring Assisted Reproductive Technologies (ICMART). 2010. "Cross-Border Fertility Care—International Committee Monitoring Assisted Reproductive Technologies Global Survey: 2006 Data and Estimates." *Fertility and Sterility* 94(1):e4–e10.

Ong, Aihwa, and Stephen J. Collier, eds. 2005. *Global Assemblages: Technology, Politics and Ethics as Anthropological Problems.* Oxford: Blackwell.

Pande, Amrita. 2015. "Blood, Sweat and Dummy Tummies: Kin Labour and Transnational Surrogacy in India." *Anthropologica* 57(1):53–62.

Park, Kristin. 2002. "Stigma Management amongst the Voluntary Childless." *Sociological Perspectives* 45(1):21–45.

Pennings, Guido. 2002. "Reproductive Tourism as Moral Pluralism in Motion." *Journal of Medical Ethics* 28(6):337–341.

———. 2005. "Reply to 'Reproductive Exile versus Reproductive Tourism.'" *Human Reproduction.* 20(12):3571–3572.

Petryna, Adriana. 2003. *Life Exposed: Biological Citizens after Chernobyl*. Princeton, NJ: Princeton University Press.

Polat, Nurhak. 2012. "Concerned Groups in the Field of Reproductive Technologies: A Turkish Case." Pp. 197–228 in *Reproductive Technologies as Global Form: Ethnographies of Knowledge, Practices, and Transnational Encounters*, edited by Michi Knecht, Maren Klotz, and Stefan Beck. Frankfurt: Campus Verlag.

Prainsack, Barbara. 2014. "The Powers of Participatory Medicine." *PLOS Biology* 12(4):e1001837.

Price, Frances. 1999. "Triplets: Who Cares?" Pp. 49–60 in *Extending the Boundaries of Care: Medical Ethics and Caring Practices*, edited by Tamara Kohn and Rosemary McKechnie. London: Bloomsbury Academic.

Rabinow, Paul. 1996. *Making PCR: A Story of Biotechnology*. Chicago: University of Chicago Press.

Ragoné, Heléna. 2005. "Surrogate Motherhood: Rethinking Biological Models, Kinship and Family." Pp. 471–480 in *Gender in Cross-Cultural Perspective*, edited by Caroline B. Brettell and Carolyn F. Sargent. 4th ed. Upper Saddle River, NJ: Prentice-Hall.

Rapp, Rayna. 2000. *Testing Women, Testing the Fetus: The Social Impact of Amniocentesis in America*. New York: Routledge.

Roberts, Elizabeth F. S. 2008. "Biology, Sociality and Reproductive Modernity in Ecuadorian In-Vitro Fertilization: The Particulars of Place." Pp. 79–97 in *Biosocialities, Genetics and the Social Sciences: Making Biologies and Identities*, edited by Sarah Gibbon and Carlos Novas. New York: Routledge.

Rose, Nikolas. 2007. *The Politics of Life Itself: Biomedicine, Power, and Subjectivity in the Twenty-First Century*. Princeton, NJ: Princeton University Press.

Rose, Nikolas, and Carlos Novas. 2005. "Biological Citizenship." Pp. 439–463 in *Global Assemblages: Technology, Politics, and Ethics as Anthropological Problems*, edited by Aihwa Ong and Stephen J. Collier. Oxford: Blackwell.

Rosenfeld, Dana, and Christopher A. Faircloth. 2006. *Medicalized Masculinities*. Philadelphia: Temple University Press.

Rothman, Barbara Katz. 2004. "Caught in the Current." Pp. 279–288 in *Consuming Motherhood*, edited by Janelle S. Taylor, Linda L. Layne, and Danielle F. Wozniak. Piscataway, NJ: Rutgers University Press.

———. 2005. *Weaving a Family: Untangling Race and Adoption*. Boston: Beacon Press.

———. 2006. "Adoption and the Culture of Genetic Determinism." Pp. 19–28 in *Adoptive Families in a Diverse Society*, edited by Katarina Wegar. Piscataway, NJ: Rutgers University Press.

Sandelowski, Margarete. 1990. "Fault Lines: Infertility and Imperiled Sisterhood." *Feminist Studies* 16(1):33–51.

———. 1991. "Compelled to Try: The Never Enough Quality of Conceptive Technology." *Medical Anthropology Quarterly*. 5(1):29–47.

Slepičková, Lenka, and Petr Fučík. 2009. "The Social Context of Attitudes toward Various Infertility Strategies." *Czech Sociological Review* 45(2):267–290.

Smith, Dorothy E. 1993. "The Standard North American Family: SNAF as an Ideological Code." *Journal of Family Issues* 14(1):50–65.

Snodgrass, Jeffrey G., H. J. François Dengah, and Michael G. Lacy. 2014. "'I Swear to God, I Only Want People Here Who Are Losers!' Cultural Dissonance and the (Problematic) Allure of *Azeroth.*" *Medical Anthropology Quarterly* 28(4):480–501.

Snowden, Robert, G. D. Mitchell, and E. M. Snowden. 1983. *Artificial Reproduction: A Social Investigation.* London: Unwin Hyman.

Sobo, Elisa, Elizabeth Herlihy, and Mary Bicker. 2011. "Selling Medical Travel to US Patient- Consumers: The Cultural Appeal of Website Marketing Messages." *Anthropology and Medicine* 18(1):119–136.

Solinger, Barbara. 2002. *Beggars and Choosers: How the Politics of Choice Shapes Adoption, Abortion, and Welfare in the United States.* New York: Hill and Wang.

Spar, Debora. 2006. *The Baby Business: How Money, Science, and Politics Drive the Commerce of Conception.* Boston: Harvard Business School Press.

Spar, Debora, and Anna Harrington. 2009. "Building a Better Baby Business." *Minnesota Journal of Law, Science and Technology* 10(1):41–69.

Speier, Amy. 2011a. "Brokers, Consumers, and the Internet: How North American Consumers Navigate Their Infertility Journeys." *Reproductive BioMedicine Online* 23(5):592–599.

———. 2011b. "'IVF Holiday': Contradictions of Patient Care Abroad." *CARGO: Journal for Cultural and Social Anthropology* 9(1–2):7–24.

———. 2012. "Reproductive Tourism: Health Care Crisis Reifies Globalized Stratified Reproduction." Pp. 209–226 in *Global Tourism: Cultural Heritage and Economic Encounters*, edited by Sarah M. Lyon and E. Christian Wells. Lanham, MD: AltaMira Press.

———. 2015. "Czech Hosts Creating 'A Real Home away from Home' for North American Reproductive Tourists." *Anthropologica* 57(1):27–40.

Stone, Linda. 2014. *Kinship and Gender: An Introduction.* 5th ed. Boulder, CO: Westview Press.

Strathern, Marilyn. 2005. *Kinship, Law and the Unexpected: Relatives Are Always a Surprise.* Cambridge: Cambridge University Press.

Sundby, Johanne. 2002. "Infertility and Health Care in Countries with Less Resources: Case Studies from Sub-Saharan Africa." Pp. 247–260 in *Infertility around the Globe: New Thinking on Childlessness, Gender and Reproductive Technologies*, edited by Marcia C. Inhorn and Frank van Balen. Berkeley: University of California Press.

Thompson, Charis. 2005. *Making Parents: The Ontological Choreography of Reproductive Technologies.* Boston: MIT Press.

Thompson, William, and Joseph V. Hickey. 2005. *Society in Focus.* Boston: Pearson.

Throsby, Karen. 2004. *When IVF Fails: Feminism, Infertility and the Negotiation of Normality.* New York: Palgrave Macmillan.

Tober, Diane M. 2002. "Semen as Gift, Semen as Goods: Reproductive Workers and the Market in Altruism." Pp. 137–160 in *Commodifying Bodies*, edited by Nancy Scheper-Hughes and Loïc Wacquant. London: Sage.

Turiel, Judith Steinberg. 1998. *Beyond Second Opinions: Making Choices about Fertility Treatment*. Berkeley: University of California Press.

United Nations. 2015. "The Universal Declaration of Human Rights." http://www.un.org/en/documents/udhr/.

Urry, John. 2002. *The Tourist Gaze*. 2nd ed. London: Sage.

van Balen, Frank, and Marcia C. Inhorn. 2002. "Introduction. Interpreting Infertility: A View from the Social Sciences." Pp. 3–32 in *Infertility around the Globe: New Thinking on Childlessness, Gender and Reproductive Technologies*, edited by Marcia C. Inhorn and Frank van Balen. Berkeley: University of California Press.

Waldby, Catherine, and Robert Mitchell. 2006. *Tissue Economies: Blood, Organs, and Cell Lines in Late Capitalism*. Durham, NC: Duke University Press.

Whittaker, Andrea. 2008. "Pleasure and Pain: Medical Travel in Asia." *Global Public Health: An International Journal for Research, Policy and Practice* 3(3):271–290.

———. 2011. "Cross-Border Assisted Reproductive Care in Asia: Implications for Access, Equity and Regulations." *Reproductive Health Matters* 19(37):107–116.

Whittaker, Andrea, Lenore Manderson, and Elizabeth Cartwright. 2010. "Patients without Borders: Understanding Medical Travel." *Medical Anthropology: Cross Cultural Studies in Health and Illness* 29(4):336–343.

Whittaker, Andrea, and Amy Speier. 2010. "'Cycling Overseas': Care, Commodification, and Stratification in Cross-Border Reproductive Travel." *Medical Anthropology* 29(4):363–383.

Whyte, Susan Reynolds, Sjaak van der Geest, and Anita Hardon. 2003. *Social Lives of Medicines*. Cambridge: Cambridge University Press.

Zanini, Giulia. 2011. "Abandoned by the State, Betrayed by the Church: Italian Experiences of Cross-Border Reproductive Care." *Reproductive BioMedicine Online* 23(5):565–572.

INDEX

adoption, 28, 29, 133, 142; international, 127, 136

affective discourse, 15, 65, 91, 106

alienation, 15, 36–38

anonymous egg donation, 5, 6, 64, 68, 72–75, 84, 132, 149

assisted reproductive technologies, 1, 7, 26, 81, 121, 122, 128; as addictive, 29, 109; of Czech Republic, 63; consumer demand for, 26; ethical dimensions, 27; feminist response to, 9; high cost, 4; investment, 123; regulations of, 5

baby as souvenir, 123, 142, 143

"baby business," 7, 14, 17–18, 32, 37–39, 41, 137, 147, 149

bioavailability, 64

biological citizenship, 14–15; digital, 43; global, 42–43

biological privilege, 127

biomedical self-shaping, 99

biomedicalization, 43

biosocial community, 43–44, 62, 116, 149; gendered, 44, 46–48; virtual, 15, 44, 92, 95, 97, 105, 141, 142; virtual as gendered, 141, 142, 147

biosociality, 90

body as private property, 20

Brno, 10, 66, 92, 96

Brown, Louise, 63

care, 40, 45, 57, 60–61, 65, 76, 85, 87, 89, 92, 105, 106, 122, 137, 147, 148; lack of, 37–38; marketing, 53–56

chemical pregnancy, 30

children born of third party donation, 132, 146; mental health, 133

Clomid, 30, 33

clone, 127–128

complicated pregnancy, 15

compulsion to try, 17, 25, 27–28, 30, 107, 122, 132, 137, 139, 145

connections, 61

contradiction, 8, 9, 15, 17, 19, 102, 103, 116, 117, 147, 149; of assisted reproductive technologies, 27; of Internet, 43, 48

cross-border reproductive care. *See* reproductive travel

cultural script, 17, 27; of health, 21; lack of for infertility, 25

Czech clinic, 11, 15, 52–54, 56, 57, 62, 63, 65, 66, 67, 78–79, 87, 89, 93, 95, 98, 100, 102, 116, 119, 137, 149; website, 6, 66, 71, 100

Czech clinic coordinator, 90–91, 92–93, 100; gendered, 91

Czech egg donors, 53, 56, 66, 71, 74, 81, 84, 129; white, 7–8, 80, 83, 84, 127, 129, 147

Czech legislation, 64, 68, 73, 76, 121

Czech Republic, 2–3, 51, 102, 149

depression, 17, 23

disclosure/non-disclosure, 127, 132, 133, 134, 135, 136, 142

egg retrieval, 112

embryo adoption, 34

embryo freezing, 35, 112, 114, 137, 139, 142

embryo transfer, 27, 29, 88, 89, 102, 113, 114, 115, 116, 142, 145
epigenetics, 130–131
ethics, 138; dilemmas, 142; genealogical, 131
Europe as racialized, 80

failed performance, 89–90
fertility holiday, 7, 15, 57, 62, 102, 103, 116, 147, 148, 150; branding, 45, 51, 100, 109; as cost effective, 59
fertility journey, 14, 19, 103, 121; consumer element of, 96
fertility threads, 46, 48
fertility tourism. *See* reproductive travel
foster care, 142, 146

gambling, 17, 19, 30, 31, 109, 114, 124–125
gender, 1, 11, 25, 31, 48
genetics, 81, 83–84, 128, 129
global assemblage, 99
global care chain, 7, 15, 52, 57, 89, 91, 95, 100, 104, 105
global market of healthcare, 6, 48, 56, 129, 137, 146, 147, 148
Google, 10, 41, 43, 49, 50, 148

health as commodity, 41
health insurance, 144
heritage tours, 136
hope, 3, 17, 45–46, 48, 51, 61–62, 63, 101, 103, 115, 137; diaspora of, 147; ideology, 24; technologies, 7, 9, 15

ICSI, 32, 35, 145, 151n1
individual responsibility, 14, 18–19, 21–23, 27–28, 42–43, 49, 97, 103, 108, 114, 115, 130, 147, 148
infertility, 1, 14, 19, 34, 56, 60, 130, 147; causes of, 21, 33, 108; as gendered, 21, 46–47, 62
insurance, 34–35
Internet, 15, 41, 43, 46–47, 90, 95, 98, 132, 146, 147, 148; as source of information, 49, 50, 96, 148

"interracial surveillance," 127
"intimate labor," 15, 45, 60–61, 65, 76–77, 84, 86, 100, 104, 117, 122, 148, 149
IUI, 1, 26, 29, 30, 31, 33, 35
IVF, 1, 26, 29, 30, 33, 39, 65; cost, 6, 33, 35–36, 37, 56, 72, 103, 123, 145; failed cycle, 12, 24, 38, 119, 123, 149; "technology of racism," 56
IVF broker, 2, 7, 10, 23, 38, 45, 57–58, 60–61, 77–79, 87, 89, 91, 92, 93, 95, 96, 97, 100, 101, 111, 124, 134, 142, 148, 149; branding, 9, 15; "interface agents," 44; IVF choices, 51–52, 58, 65, 67, 74, 92, 95, 138; IVF holiday, 2, 10, 35, 51–52, 56, 57, 65, 67, 76, 91, 92, 93, 99, 104, 110; websites, 44–45, 50–54, 59, 61, 63, 78, 148
IVF using egg donor, 5, 13, 27, 29, 58, 74, 79, 81, 82, 83, 84, 100, 119, 121, 127, 128, 129, 132, 135, 142

kinship, 7, 61, 121; commodification of, 123; cultures or geographies of relatedness, 81, 117, 140–141; heteronormative families, 6, 46, 68, 121, 122, 123; ideal family, 121, 128; "natural" family, 128; "normal," 134; "passing," 127
kinship work, 43; as gendered, 122, 141, 147

lay referral group, 44, 62
"logic of choice," 49

matching, 82
medicalized reproduction, 26
methodology, 10
miscarriage, 33, 114, 115, 142, 144
multiple pregnancy, 3, 15, 29, 34, 52, 114, 115, 118, 123, 124, 125, 132, 135, 140, 141, 142, 144, 145, 149

natural conception, 20, 26
neoliberal discourse, 56
neoliberal healthcare, 7, 8, 16, 32, 41–43, 65, 76, 86, 99, 100, 147
neoliberal market conditions, 18–19, 105

"open" egg donation, 131
ovarian hyperstimulation syndrome, 75

parenthood, 17; gendered, 132; healthy, 134; timing of, 20–21
patient activism, 96, 97, 98, 99, 149
patient as consumer, 8, 9, 13, 18, 40, 42, 50, 54–55, 62, 87–88, 89, 114, 137, 147, 148, 149
patient-centered care, 15, 64, 85, 89
patient empowerment, 42, 86–89
pension, 1–2, 10–11, 15, 19, 104–106, 116, 123, 124, 119, 149
PGD, 5, 69, 99
physician authority, 38–39
Pilka, Ladislav, 63, 66, 70
political economies of hope, 7, 148
polycystic ovarian syndrome, 33
positive thinking, 17, 24, 103, 110, 115, 147; discourse, 149; ideology, 108, 116; moral axiom, 29
pregnancy, 121, 129, 130, 134
premature birth, 143, 144
procreative tourism. *See* reproductive travel
professional guinea pig, 31, 114
psychological testing, 24

quest for parenthood, 6, 43, 55, 118, 121

race/ethnicity, 8, 79, 127
recombinant families, 121
reproductive exile, 4, 36, 101
reproductive medicine, commercialization of, 4, 27, 32
reproductive trafficking. *See* reproductive travel
reproductive travel, 3, 103; as gendered, 147; hubs, 5–6, 149; marketed via the Internet, 43; routes, 5–6; terms, 4
reproductive travelers, 11, 13–14, 86, 89, 100, 117, 123; community of, 106; lower middle class, 13; term, 101

resemblance, 7, 81–83, 121, 126, 127, 128, 129, 131
RESOLVE (support group), 1–2, 95–96
return reproductive travel, 7, 16, 60, 106, 108, 117, 122, 126, 137, 138, 139, 142, 145, 149
rights discourse, 20, 131; rights of children, 131; right to parent, 133, 134
risk taking, 31

Skype, 24, 50, 58–59, 95, 119, 138
social kinship, 15, 106, 117, 122, 123, 139, 140, 141, 149; as gendered, 122; gifts that sustain, 142
social media, 12, 15, 50, 93, 126, 142, 149; as gendered, 46, 62
social norm, 17, 19, 20
stigma, 17, 21, 24, 29, 74, 106, 133–134, 144, 147; of trying too hard, 24
stratified reproduction, 9, 64, 100
stress, 43, 45, 57, 59, 61, 83, 102, 108, 110, 112, 113, 116, 149; and infertility, 23; of IVF, 53–54
suffering, 17, 25
support group, 1, 2, 46, 95–96, 97–98, 99; virtual, 148
surrogacy, 5, 27, 30, 69–70, 130

testimonials, 2, 50, 53–56, 59, 61, 97, 101, 104, 109, 116, 150
tourist imagination, 45, 147

vacation, 4, 116; branding, 4; ensures successful IVF, 111; European, 7, 53, 60–61, 101, 147, 148; as ideology, 9; interrupted, 103, 112, 113, 116, 150; "vacationscapes," 45
virtual communities, 65, 122

work ethic, 17, 40, 48, 50, 56, 62, 108, 111, 116, 121, 122, 129, 131, 134, 137, 147; discourse, 125, 149; ideology, 19, 28

Zlín, 10, 19, 67, 73, 93, 94, 95, 96, 98, 99, 104, 105, 106, 113, 118, 133, 137, 140

ABOUT THE AUTHOR

Amy Speier has been conducting ethnographic fieldwork in the Czech Republic for more than a decade, examining various realms of medical tourism. Dr. Speier has lived all over the United States, and her nomadic life instilled her love of anthropology and travel. She currently lives in Fort Worth, Texas.